D1153958

Information Storage and Retrieval
Systems for Individual Researchers

Information Sciences Series

Information Storage and Retrieval Systems for Individual Researchers

Gerald Jahoda

SCHOOL OF LIBRARY SCIENCE
FLORIDA STATE UNIVERSITY

Wiley-Interscience

Division of John Wiley & Sons

NEW YORK · LONDON · SYDNEY · TORONTO

To

GLORIA

*for her encouragement and help above
and beyond the call of wifely duty*

Information Sciences Series

Information is the essential ingredient in decision making. The need for improved information systems in recent years has been made critical by the steady growth in size and complexity of organizations and data.

This series is designed to include books that are concerned with various aspects of communicating, utilizing, and storing digital and graphic information. It will embrace a broad spectrum of topics, such as information system theory and design, man-machine relationships, language data processing, artificial intelligence, mechanization of library processes, non-numerical applications of digital computers, storage and retrieval, automatic publishing, command and control, information display, and so on.

Information science may someday be a profession in its own right. The aim of this series is to bring together the interdisciplinary core of knowledge that is apt to form its foundation. Through this consolidation, it is expected that the series will grow to become the focal point for professional education in this field.

Preface

What researcher has not looked through his files for a report or other document that he knows is in his office but that he cannot locate? If such a loss of a document is infrequent and temporary (that is, the document usually shows up when something else is sought) and the result is only some minor frustration, inconvenience, or embarrassment, it is usually accepted as one of the world's imperfections; nothing is done about it. If, on the other hand, such occurrences are both frequent and more than a minor source of inconvenience (these are subjective factors to be weighed by each reader), improvements in memory, information gathering habits, or the document retrieval system are probably worth consideration.

This book deals with the simplest of the three corrective measures—the improvement of the document retrieval system. There are different ways and means of accomplishing this, and these methods of improving the organization and retrieval of personal document collections are the principal topics to be covered. The book is addressed primarily to the researcher in any subject field who desires to improve the index to his document collection or start an index to his document collection but does not quite know how to go about it. An index is herein defined as a systematic organization of a collection of documents or data. There are indexes to various types of document and data collections, and there are various types of indexes. Examples of familiar indexes are indexes to individual books, to collections of books (the card catalog in a library), to the contents of journals or periodicals (for example, the *Reader' Guide to Periodical Literature*), to collections of facts (for example, a telephone directory), or to numeric data (such as physical constants of a group of compounds or numeric data collected in a questionnaire study).

This book will be concerned primarily with indexes to collections of documents in researchers' offices. Documents are defined broadly as physical marks on paper, film, or glass that the researcher refers to with enough frequency during the course of his work to warrant keeping them in his office. Such document collections may include journal articles, reports, theses, books, parts of books, letters, lecture notes, maps, graphs, and drawings. The collections of documents in researchers offices vary in size depending on the researchers' breadth of interest, memory, the number of years they have been active as researchers, and probably many other factors. In a recent survey of researchers in the sciences and engineering at one university, the size of personal indexes ranged from several hundred to 10,000 documents.* Indexes will be discussed in terms of this range of document numbers, since it is assumed that smaller collections are not likely to require much in the way of an index and much larger collections might warrant the use of more sophisticated schemes.

There are different types of indexes, and the individual indexes belonging to a particular type can also differ from one another. An analogy may be drawn from the automotive industry. You may have the same make of car as your neighbor, but yours may be equipped with a "four-on-the-floor" transmission whereas the neighbor's car has an automatic transmission. The same type of index can also come with different types of accessories or equivalents thereof depending on your needs, habits, or inclinations. We can look at ways of organizing collections of documents as a spectrum. On one end of the spectrum we find the so-called "woman's handbag" method of organization, or more precisely, lack of organization. To find what you want, empty the handbag, or in our case look at every single document to determine whether or not it is relevant to your question. At the other end of the spectrum we have the push-button system. Here by some form of magic as yet out of our reach except for demonstrations you push one or a small number of buttons and the relevant documents appear before you on a television-like screen without delay.† We shall largely ignore the ends of this spectrum and concentrate on methods of organization that have been used for document collections within the specified orders of magnitude.

It gives me pleasure to acknowledge the assistance of a number of people and organizations. I would like to thank Mrs. Joan Chellis for her superb job of typing from a hard-to-read manuscript and also for the

---

* Jahoda, G., Hutchins, R. D. and Galford, R. R., "Characteristics and Use of Personal Indexes Maintained by Scientists and Researchers in One University," *American Documentation,* **17**:71–75 (1966).

† One of the most widely quoted and most influential articles on push-button information systems was written by Vannevar Bush, a prominent American scientist. Some but not all of the features of Bush's predicted information systems are available today. Bush V., "As We May Think," *Atlantic Monthly.* **176**:101–108 (July 1945).

preparation of the illustrations. Helpful comments were received from my students at the Florida State University School of Library Science. Thanks are due to the Gulf Publishing Company, the IBM Corporation, the National Academy of Sciences—National Research Council, the New York Times, and Science Service for permission to reproduce material for illustration. Finally, to my wife for her generous help in editing and proofing the manuscript.

GERALD JAHODA

Tallahassee, Florida
September, 1969

Contents

Information Storage and Retrieval
Systems for Individual Researchers

Chapter One

A Preliminary Look at Indexes

Let us look at three types of indexes, mostly to become acquainted with the terminology and to introduce a variable or two. We will assume that the brief article from *Science News* reproduced in Figure 1-1 is one article that we wish to include in our personal document collection. The size and content of the document were chosen for convenience and to make some points. It could have been a lengthy report, a conference paper, a slide, or any other document. The document consists of a text and a bibliographic citation. The bibliographic citation is made up in this example of the title of the document, the name of the journal, the journal volume, the page of the journal, and the year of publication. The author is not identified in this particular case. The bibliographic citation serves as a representation of the document and is used as such when the document is referred to in another publication, whether this publication is another journal article, an index, or anything else. There is no other document with the same bibliographic citation, hence the bibliographic citation is a unique means for document identification. (Some readers may prefer a conditional "should be" to the more definite "is" statement about unique identification of document if they have encountered the same article in more than one publication or if they had the bibliographic citation but could not locate the document. These

RADIOACTIVE DATING. ART WORKS DATED ATOMICALLY

Radioactive dating of works of art by measuring the alpha particles emitted by the lead contained in the paint, pewter or bronze has been found a valuable way of distinguishing between originals and forgeries.

Scientific tools of increasing sensitivity and sophistication have been used to examine the materials of art and archaeology and to support judgments concerning authenticity. However, as forgers become acquainted with new methods, they learn how to circumvent them.

No circumvention is possible with the method based on detection of radioactive lead 210, since it disintegrates with a half-life of 22 years unless its long-lived precursor, radium 226, is present.

The catch is that the radium is separated chemically from lead when lead and its products are prepared from the ore.

The paint sample must be white lead of high purity for the method to work, Dr. Bernard Keisch, now of Mellon Institute in Pittsburgh, and his co-workers there and at Nuclear Science and Engineering Corporation, Pittsburgh, report in the March 10 SCIENCE.

The method has been suggested and tested previously but no instruments capable of distinguishing between the concentrations of radium 226 and its descendants were available then.
Science News, **91**:284 (1967).

Figure 1-1.   Sample document for indexing.

problems are acknowledged but considered outside the scope of our discussion.)

When a document is referred to in an index, the bibliographic citation is augmented with a word or a phrase. This word or phrase is chosen to characterize an aspect or portion of the document or the entire document. The word or phrase may identify a subject discussed in the document; it may identify *the* subject if only one subject is discussed or if the user of the index is only interested in one of several subjects discussed. The word or phrase may also represent the author or the author's professional affiliation. This word or phrase is called the index heading. The index heading and the unique identification of the document make up the index entry. Figure 1-2 illustrates possible index entries for the document reproduced in Figure 1-1. We will refer a number of times to this document and call it the radioactive dating document.

The index entries illustrated in Figure 1-2 are examples of a widely used type of index called the alphabetic subject index. The dots between entries are intended to indicate that these entries are interfiled with entries for other documents. You have encountered this type of index in your use of the card catalog in the library or the *Readers' Guide to Periodical Literature*. One characteristic of this index is that the individual index entries are arranged in one alphabet by the first word of the index heading. Several index entries have been selected for the radioactive dating document and there are at least two reasons for this. First, the index entry in this type of index can only be located under the first word of the index heading. The index headings "Alpha radiation measurement in lead 210" and "Lead 210, alpha radiation measurement"

Alpha radiation measurement in lead 210
  "Radioactive dating. Art works dated atomically," *Science News*, **91**:284 (1967).
  .
  .
  .

Bronze, radioactive dating
  "Radioactive dating. Art works dated atomically," *Science News*, **91**:284 (1967).
  .
  .
  .

Lead 210, alpha radiation measurement
  "Radioactive dating. Art works dated atomically," *Science News*, **91**:284 (1967).
  .
  .
  .

Paintings, radioactive dating
  "Radioactive dating. Art works dated atomically," *Science News*, **91**:284 (1967).
  .
  .
  .

Pewter, radioactive dating
  "Radioactive dating. Art works dated atomically," *Science News*, **91**:284 (1967).
  .
  .
  .

Radioactive dating of art works containing lead
  "Radoactive dating. Art works dated atomically," *Science News*, **91**:284 (1967).

Figure 1-2.   Alphabetic subject index entries.

consist of the same words. The order of the words has been changed in the second entry so that the searcher can locate this document under the word "Lead 210." Notice that no index heading starts with the word "measurement" which means that this document cannot be located under this word. The second reason for having more than one index entry for a document is that the document may deal with more than one topic that needs to be brought to the attention of future users of the index. Not all of the topics discussed in this article have been characterized as index entries. For example, nothing was said about radium 226 or about Dr. Bernard Keisch, although we could have made entries for either or both of these aspects of the document. A choice has to be made by the indexer of topics in a particular document as to what to include in the index. Another choice or decision needs to be made as to how the index headings are to be phrased. For example, the index heading "Alpha radiation in lead 210" could also have been worded this way: "Alpha particles count in lead 210." The number of index entries per document varies from document to document depending upon its importance to the individual researcher, the number of documents on the topic in his collection, and the amount of time he wants to take for this task, to mention several factors. The average number of index entries per document in a collection is characteristic of a factor called the depth of the index. Indexing depth may average one or two entries per document or it may average 10 or more entries per document. Indexing depth and index vocabulary (the words and phrases used in index headings) are discussed in some detail in later chapters.

In an alphabetic subject index, the first word in an index heading is the access point for that index heading. The word "measurement" is not an access point in our example, as was already pointed out, because no index heading begins with this word. The alphabetic subject index can only be searched under the first words of index headings selected at the time of indexing. Also, the index heading is the word or combination of words selected at the time of indexing. Thus the index heading and the search heading are one and the same in the alphabetic subject index. This is not so for the coordinate index, as we shall now see.

Figure 1-3 gives the coordinate index entries for the radioactive dating document. Again each beginning word or only word in the index heading is the access point for this document. The coordinate index, unlike the alphabetic subject index, can also be searched under *any combination of index headings* that were selected at the time of indexing. For example, the radioactive dating document can be located by searching for *radioactive dating* of *lead 210* in *pewters*. The coordinate index

Alpha radiation	Paintings
245	245
Bronze	Pewter
245	245
Lead 210	Radioactive dating
245	245
Measurement	
245	

Figure 1-3.   Coordinate index entries.

headings which are combined or coordinated for this search are in italics. One more difference between the illustrated alphabetic subject index and coordinate index headings needs to be pointed out before we can show how searches are conducted in coordinate indexes. In the alphabetic subject index we used the bibliographic citation as the unique identification of a document. In most coordinate indexes a unique accession number for a document in a given index serves the same purpose. This accession number is called the document number. The document number is easier to manipulate than the bibliographic citation in searching the index.

The index heading in a coordinate index goes under several names: aspect, uniterm, concept, descriptor. We shall call it descriptor. The index entry in the illustrated coordinate index is made up of the descriptor and the document number. The coordinate index may be prepared in various physical forms. In the example given in Figure 1-4, one card is made for each descriptor. On this descriptor card are posted the document numbers that have as one of their descriptors the descriptor listed on that card. The document numbers are arranged by terminal digit (all numbers ending with 0 are in the 0 column, all document numbers ending with a 1 are in the 1 column, etc.) and in ascending numeric order. Searching this form of coordinate index consists of looking for common document numbers on two descriptor cards. If the search involves the coordination of three descriptors, one takes the common numbers found in matching the first two descriptor cards and matches these numbers against the numbers on the third descriptor card. This process is continued with as many descriptor cards as are necessary. In the example given in Figure 1-4, document numbers 187, 245, and 320 are common to both descriptor cards. This means that these three documents are each indexed under the descriptors "Paintings" and "Radioactive dating." If a third descriptor, say "Lead 210," had to be searched, the presence of document numbers 187, 245, and 320 would

Paintings

0	1	2	3	4	5	6	7	8	9
110	311	102	233	444	125		127	138	189
280	421	152	343		185		(187)	228	
(320)		362			(245)		217	248	
490					285		247		

Radioactive dating

0	1	2	3	4	5	6	7	8	9
150	121	132	143	124	(245)	156	137		149
240	151	182	173	164	265	216	157		219
290	191	252	253	594	295	266	(187)		249
(320)	211	282	283				227		269
	421								309

Figure 1-4. Descriptor cards.

be checked on the "Lead 210" descriptor card. Notice that the arrangement of the document numbers by terminal digits and in ascending order facilitates the number matching operation. There are other forms of coordinate indexes and these are discussed in a later chapter.

A third type of index is illustrated in Figure 1-5. This is an example of a keyword from title index, specifically the keyword-in-context or KWIC index, and is called this for reasons that will shortly become apparent. As in the case of the coordinate index, the document is identified uniquely by means of a document number. (This is not always the practice for either the coordinate or KWIC index and later we shall show examples of these types of indexes that provide more meaningful identifying information per document.) The index entry for the KWIC index again consists of the index heading and the document identification, in this case the document number. In Figure 1-5, the individual entries are separated by dots to indicate that the entries for this document are interfiled with entries for other documents. The index heading of the KWIC index is usually the title of the document. Multiple index headings are obtained for each title by filing the title under each of its significant words. Each significant word in a title is brought into the filing position which in this case is the center of the line rather than the more conventional left hand margin. The filing point per entry (the access point) is surrounded by the other words in the title—its context—hence the name keyword-in-context index. The individual title entries are filed alphabetically. In our example all title words were considered significant and therefore access points. Nonsignificant words as exemplified by articles, pronouns, and prepositions can be excluded as access points without excluding their presence in the title entry. In other words, nonsignificant words are omitted as filing points only but will appear in the entry at other times. The KWIC index requires little intellectual effort if it is only based on the title which, after all, is picked by the author. The title may or may not have all the important keywords that are required to represent and later search the document. In our example, we would not be able to locate the radioactive dating document under "Lead 210," "Pewter," "Paintings," nor "Bronze." There is a way of getting around this limitation. We can enrich the title with additional keywords or rewrite the title. Once again, this is a topic for discussion in a separate chapter.

Which type of index and which of the accessories, to go back to

Radioactive dating.	Art works dated atomically	245
.		
.		
.		
Art works dated	atomically. Radioactive dating	245
.		
.		
.		
dating. Art works	dated atomically. Radioactive	245
.		
.		
.		
dated atomically	Radioactive dating. Art works	245

Figure 1-5.   Keyword-in-context index entries.

the car analogy used in the preface, should the researcher select for his document or data retrieval system? This is, of course, the basic question we have to deal with. Before we go any further and raise some unjustified hopes, it might be well to point out that just as in the selection of a car, there is no unique best answer. There are too many subjective factors that cannot be measured and too many things that we do not as yet know about indexing systems. But there are guidelines that enable us to determine whether to get a Volkswagen or a Cadillac index and what accessories we should include.

The next chapter describes procedures used in the preparation of indexes and discusses variables in the preparation and use of indexes.

SUGGESTIONS FOR FURTHER READING

Becker, J. and Hayes, R. M., *Information Storage and Retrieval: Tools: Elements, Theories*, New York: Wiley, 1963.

Howerton, P., ed., *Information Handling: First Principles*. Washington, D.C.: Spartan Books, 1963.

Jonker, F., *Indexing Theory, Indexing Methods, and Search Devices*. New York: Scarecrow Press, 1964.

Kent A., *Textbook on Mechanized Information Retrieval*, 2nd ed. New York: Interscience, 1966.

Meadow, C. T., *The Analysis of Information Systems: A Programmer's Introduction to Information Retrieval*. New York: Wiley, 1967.

Chapter Two

Basic Aspects of Index Use and Preparation

Before we discuss the steps in preparing an index, we will go through the steps in using an index. Let us, therefore, assume that we need to conduct a subject search in an index. We will take a relatively simple example but one not without some complications. The complications have been selected to illustrate problems in both searching and preparing indexes. Our hypothetical search is for all journal articles on the architecture of junior colleges in the United States. The search will be conducted in one volume of the *Readers' Guide to Periodical Literature.* This is an author and subject index to over 130 general and nontechnical journals. We will search volume 25 which covers the period of March 1965 to February 1966. The principal steps in such a search are listed in the flowchart given as Figure 2-1.

We begin with a need for information on the architecture of junior colleges in the United States and assume that this need has already been translated into words. These words are usually not the words with which we can search the index as we shall see, or as the reader probably has already experienced. This second translation step requires some

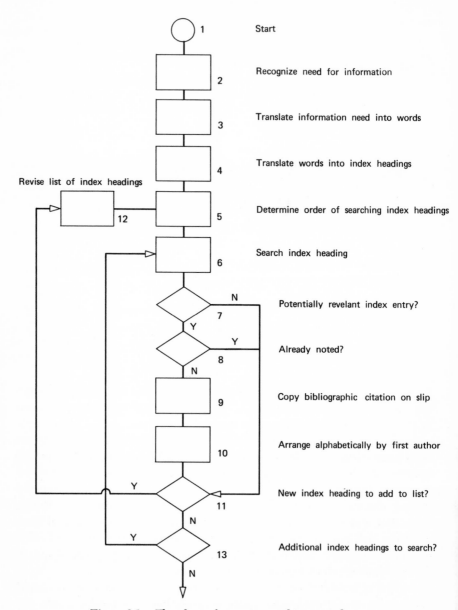

Figure 2-1. Flowchart of steps in searching an index.

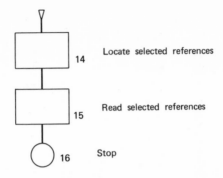

14   Locate selected references

15   Read selected references

16   Stop

Identification of symbols:

◯ = start or stop   ◇ = decision

▽ ⅄ = connector out, connector in

□ = action

——Y—— = yes line

——N—— = no line

Figure 2-1. (*Continued*).

familiarity with the index. If we compile a list of index (search) headings rather than a single heading, and this is usually the case, we will have to decide in what order the individual index headings are to be searched. The search order and the list of index headings are usually revised during the course of the search as we learn more about the index and also more about what we are looking for. In this index (illustrated in Figure 2-2), the complete bibliographic citation for every cited document is given under each index heading. (This is not the case with all indexes. In some, only serial numbers or other codes are listed under the index headings and these numbers or codes have to be looked up in another list to get the document citation.) We look under our first index heading and copy the citation of potentially relevant documents. The documents are called potentially relevant since one cannot usually tell whether the document is relevant or not until the document

READERS' GUIDE TO PERIODICAL LITERATURE March 1965–February 1966

COLLEGE architecture
Architecture and art building will introduce Netsch's new geometries. il Arch Forum 123:42-3 S '65
Architecture that transforms a campus; Clark university. il Arch Rec 137:157-68 My '65
✓Building types study. il Arch Rec 137:143-66 Je: 138:137-60 O '65
Campus City. Chicago: University of Illinois' new urban campus. il Arch Forum 123:21-45 S '65
Container to fit the contained: new building for Harvard graduate school of education. il Time 87:64-6 Ja 21 '66
Harvard tweed: Roy E. Larsen Hall. il Newsweek 66:94 O 11 '65
Horrors at Berkeley, or did architecture make students riot? F. MacShane. il Art N 64:30-3+ S '65
In Canada, the continent's first single-structure campus. D. Lyndon. il Arch Forum 123:13-21 D '65

✓Integrated site planning and design for a small college; Concordia Lutheran Junior college, Ann Arbor, Mich. il Arch Rec 138:189-96 S '65
Ivyless halls of Yale. il Holiday 37:76-81 My '65
Labor and material required for college housing. S. F. Miller. il Mo Labor R 88:1100-4 S '65
Late Frank Lloyd Wright is completed in Kansas; Corbin education center. Wichita state U. il Fortune 71:186 Je '65
New kind of client with $1.5 billion to spend: New York state university construction fund. W. McQuade. il Fortune 71:165-6 Mr '65
✓New look of campus living. R. C. Weaver. il Am Ed 1:14-21 D '64
University building by a master hand; Alvar Aalto's new classroom complex for the Finnish technical institute, Helsinki; with commentary by F. Guthelm. il Arch Rec 137:169-76 Ap '65
See also
Dormitories
Gymnasiums

Figure 2-2. Excerpt from *Readers' Guide to Periodical Literature.*

itself is examined. It is good practice to copy each citation on a slip of paper and arrange these slips alphabetically by author or by title for the anonymous documents. In this way, the same citation (which might be found several times under several index headings) will not be copied again. At the end of the list of citations under an index heading one may find leads to additional index headings in the form of "see also" cross-references. When additional index headings to be searched are found through this or other means, the headings are added to the list and the order of searching the list of index headings might be revised. This process of searching under index headings, copying potentially relevant document citations, adding to the list of index headings, is continued until all the selected index headings have been searched. The potentially relevant documents are then scanned to eliminate the nonrelevant documents, and the remaining documents are read. This completes the general description of the subject search.

We will now follow our search for articles on architecture in United States junior colleges from steps 4 to 15 on the flowchart. Our preliminary list of index headings consists of the following two headings:

Junior colleges
Architecture—U.S.

Under "Junior colleges" we find the following potentially relevant document:

Community college provides campus plan for two year program; Henry Ford Community College, Dearborn, Michigan.
Arch. Rec. 137:184–86 (March, 1965).

This citation is copied on a slip of paper. No potentially relevant documents were found under the "Architecture—U.S." heading but the following index headings were located as useful cross-references:

College architecture
Laboratories—architecture
Library architecture

This calls for a revision of the list of index headings to be searched, namely the addition of these three new headings. The "College architecture" heading was searched next. This heading and its cited documents are reproduced as Figure 2-2. The four potentially relevant documents are marked with a check on Figure 2-2. Again, the citations are copied on slips. This index heading also provided two additional index headings to search, "Dormitories" and "Gymnasiums." These two headings and the two previously selected but as yet unsearched headings yielded the following three potentially relevant documents:

> Building types study: college dormitories. Arch. Rec. **138**:113–36 (August, 1965).
>
> Building types study: laboratory buildings. Arch. Rec. **38**:173–96 (November, 1965).
>
> Lorenz, J. G. and Muirhead, P. P. Campus library. Am. Ed. **1**:12–19 (May, 1965).

This completes the selection of index headings and the searches under the selected index headings. The eight potentially relevant documents are next looked at in the library. By scanning the documents we find three to be nonrelevant. The five relevant documents are read and this completes the search for our purpose.

The search is intended to illustrate several points. First and foremost, there are many ways of indexing a document. The odds are heavily against the searcher finding a perfect match between desired and provided index headings. Because the match is less than perfect in most searches and for other reasons that we will deal with subsequently, the search results are typically less than complete. We usually settle (either knowingly or unknowingly) for less than all the documents that are in the index on a particular subject and also select some nonrelevant documents along with relevant documents from the index. This is a fact of index use that we must accept at this time. The example has also shown that the searcher must interact with the index and alter the list of index headings that he selected at the beginning of the search when circumstances warrant this. This ability to interact with the index and to adjust the search strategy while the search is in progress is one of the important advantages of manual indexes. This advantage is not provided in machine searched indexes in which the entire document collection is searched before the search strategy can be revised.

We are now ready to prepare an index or at least describe in general terms how this is done. A flowchart, Figure 2-3, will again be used as an aid. To begin, documents come into the office and are scanned or read to determine whether or not they should be included in the index. Documents that fail this screening test are disposed by passing them on to colleagues, to the library, or perhaps into the wastebasket. The selected documents are then scanned or read for indexable information. Indexable information is defined as the topic or topics which serve to characterize the document in the index. In actual practice, the selection of documents and the selection of indexable information is usually done in one step. Two steps are listed in the flowchart to indicate that

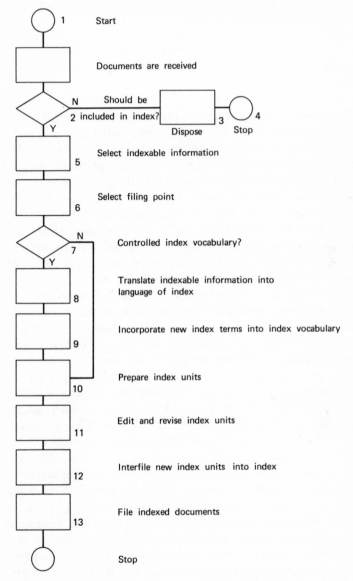

Figure 2-3. Flowchart of steps in indexing a document.

these are separate decisions even though they may be performed together. The portions of the document that are to be scanned in these two steps will depend upon how much we need to know about a document before we are ready to select or reject it and how much of the document we need to look at for the selection of indexable information. The two extreme cases for the selection of indexable information would be selection from the title only or from a reading of the entire document. The usual practice is somewhere in between. Several journals now provide indexable information with each article just as most journals now provide abstracts with each article. If the indexable information provided with the article can be used then this step is, of course, skipped. Indexable information is noted either by underlining words or phrases in the document and writing in additional words or phrases or by preparing a separate worksheet for each document. In the course of selecting indexable information for the document, the physical filing point for the document is also determined. This may be by author, under its most important subject, by date, by project, or by some number. If the document is part of a book or bound volume of a journal and the filing position is already determined, then this step is of course not applicable. The next step in indexing will differ if the index has or does not have a controlled vocabulary. For indexes with controlled vocabularies, the selected information is translated into the language of the index. It should be pointed out that a controlled index vocabulary does not mean a never-changing index vocabulary. It does mean that new terms are screened to determine if they are already covered by terms in the index (in which case the existing terms are used) and, if this is not the case, the new terms are accepted into the index once they have been defined and connected with related terms. An example of such a connection or cross-reference is given in Figure 2-2 where "College architecture" is connected to "Dormitories" and "Gymnasiums" by means of "see also" cross-references. The indexable information is therefore translated into existing indexing terms, if such terms exist or new terms are formulated, in which case the index vocabulary is revised to reflect these additions. The subsequent steps are the same for both indexes with and without controlled vocabularies. The index units are prepared. These index units for the newly indexed documents are edited and revised, if necessary. The new index units are then merged with previously prepared index units and the newly indexed documents are filed by their previously selected filing points.

This description has been kept rather general so that it can be used for various types of indexes that may differ from each other in a number of ways. For example, the physical form of the index has not been specified. It can be an index on index cards, in book form, or on tabulating or other types of cards. And the index can be an alphabetic subject index or a coordinate index.

The steps in searching and preparing an index serve as background information for the next group of topics: question variables, index variables, and the evaluation of indexes.

QUESTION VARIABLES

Let us go back to our question on the architecture of United States junior colleges to illustrate some question variables. For this question we looked in one volume of the index for all of the documents on this subject. This is not always the case. We may, for example, only want a few good documents on the subject. We may also be looking for one and only one document that we remember having seen. This would be a search for recall (for the location of something that we have seen or think that we have seen) as opposed to a search for discovery (of something that we do not know exists and may indeed not exist). We may be looking for documents, as was the case in our junior college search, or for facts or data as, for example, the population figures for a city or the boiling point of a chemical. The search for the architecture of United States junior colleges as just stated consists of seven words. Two of these words, "the" and "of," are of no value when we translate the question into the language of the index and these two words can therefore be disregarded for this purpose. The two phrases "United States" and "junior colleges" are only meaningful as phrases, not as individual words "United," "States," "junior," and "colleges" in our translation into index language step. Therefore, our question has three basic units or concepts,[2] "architecture," "United States," and "junior colleges." The number of concepts per question is another important question variable. So is the relationship among these concepts. In our search we would like to locate documents that are on a topic described by means of these three concepts. We want documents that are on architecture *and* United States *and* junior colleges. This is called a logical product search, a term borrowed from Boolean algebra.[3] Not all searches have such rigid requirements. In some searches, documents are accepted as being relevant if they deal with a topic that is characterized by some but not necessarily all of the question concepts An example of this would be a search for documents on high schools, *or* junior colleges, *or* universities. This type of question is called a logical sum question in the terminology of Boolean algebra. In the third logical type of question the presence of one or more concepts as well as the absence of one or more concepts is specified. A search for the architecture of United States junior colleges *but not* of junior colleges located in the state of New York exemplifies a logical difference search, the name given for this type of search. All questions that include more than one concept can be characterized in terms of logical product, logical sum, and logical difference searches, or as a combination of these three types of searches. (Notice that our junior college search started out as a logical product search but was reformulated into a combination of logical product and logical sum search when we translated junior college architecture as the architecture of junior colleges, or dormitories, or gymnasiums, or laboratories, or libraries.) Still another question variable is the specificity of the question. This is a relative matter. A search for the architecture of United States junior colleges is more specific than a search for the architecture of United States junior colleges and four-year colleges but less specific than a search for articles on the architecture of a specific junior college. These question variables have been introduced at this point since different types of indexes differ in their ability of handling types of questions that differ from each other in ways just discussed. References to this point will be made in chapters on types of indexes and on index design.

INDEX VARIABLES

Index variables have already been introduced in this chapter and the introductory chapter. The following discussion provides the reader with a more unified approach to this topic which should be read before going to the individual chapters on types of indexes.

Pre-Coordinated and Post-Coordinated Indexes

There are types of indexes in which the words that make up the index headings are combined (coordinated) at the time the index heading is prepared. Such indexes are called pre-coordinated indexes. The *Readers' Guide to Periodical Literature,* an alphabetic subject index, is an example of a pre-coordinated index. The *Readers' Guide* has to be searched under a combination of words selected at the time of indexing. It was not possible to search, for example, under the index heading "junior college architecture" since this phrase was not chosen as an index heading at the time of indexing. Another pre-coordinated index is the keyword-in-context index. Here again the searcher is forced to look under words or phrases selected at the time of indexing. He cannot combine these words to make index headings at the time of the search. In a post-coordinate index, usually just called coordinate index, the words and phrases selected at the time of indexing can either be searched individually or be combined at the time of searching the index as per previously discussed logical search types. Thus, had the *Readers' Guide* been a coordinate index, we might have combined the words and phrases "architecture," "United States," "junior colleges," "dormitories," "gymnasiums," "laboratories," and "libraries" into the following combination logical product and logical sum search.

Architecture and United States and either junior colleges, or dormitories, or gymnasiums, or laboratories, or libraries.

(Notice that in this search formulation we will get documents on the architecture of other than junior colleges, for example, the architecture of dormitories or gymnasiums in universities. This type of search strategy is frequently necessary to gather in documents that are not indexed in the way we would have liked to have them indexed. The penalty for this search strategy, for spreading our search net further, is that it gathers in nonrelevant documents as well as relevant documents.)

Framework for Index Vocabulary

In one type of index, the hierarchically classified index (whose relative—the Dewey Decimal Classification system—the reader probably has used), the index units have been selected before any indexing is started and the relationship among the selected index units is set in a rigid fashion or mold. This relationship is hierarchical which is an ordering of the index units starting from the very general and going to the specific with the specific always being included in the general. An example of such a hierarchy and one in a field where a hierarchy is easy to construct—this is not so of all fields—is the generic-specific relationship of the following geographic names.

North America	7
Southeastern states	75
Florida	759
Leon County	75988
Tallahassee, Florida	759881

The geographic names were translated into their Dewey Decimal Classification system numbers as a convenient number to show that all the more specific names are also coded under their more generic names.

A type of index with practically no framework is the keyword-in-context index. For this index, the index units are not selected prior to the preparation of index entries for specific documents (except in a negative way—certain nonsignificant words are excluded from indexing) and relationships among indexing units are usually not indicated. The alphabetic subject index and the coordinate index are closer to the keyword-in-context index than to the hierarchically classified index in this variable since neither type of index requires a selection of indexing terms before the index is started and in neither type of index does the relationship among indexing units have to be spelled out.

Vocabulary Control

This is a variable that is independent of the type of index except that the hierarchically classified index has its indexing language terminology rigidly controlled. The other types of indexes may range from no control to rigid control of the index vocabulary.

Types of Access Points

We have emphasized and will continue to emphasize indexing by subject because this is considered the most useful as well as difficult-to-prepare type of access point. A subject index is usually accompanied by an author index. Other access points may be by organization sponsoring the document, date of issue of document, or by serial number given to type of document exemplified by a patent or a research report.

Amount of Information Included with Each Index Unit

In the *Readers' Guide,* the full bibliographic citation of cited documents is given under each index unit. Some indexes provide more information, others provide less. Edge-notched card systems, for example, may include an abstract of the cited document or even the text of the entire document in microform with each index card. Some coordinate indexes only list serial numbers of cited documents under each index unit.

Specificity of Index Unit

This variable can be illustrated with the aid of the previously used geographic names example. If a document dealt with the city of Tallahassee, Florida, the most specific subject heading for this document would be "Tallahassee, Florida." The same subject would be indexed more generically under "Leon County, Florida," "Florida," "Southeastern states," or "United States." This is specificity of subject heading in terms of geographic name. The heading could be made more specific by including in it what is being said about Tallahassee, Florida. For example, "Tallahasseee, Florida—Architecture," or "Tallahasseee, Florida—Public school system."

Levels of Indexing

This variable characterizes the number of ways in which a particular subject described in a document is included in an index. The geographic name example will again be used. If we chose to index the geographic name as specifically as the subject permits and only in that way, then we would index on one level. Tallahassee, Florida would be indexed under "Tallahassee, Florida." We may decide to index this subject specifically as well as under one or several more generic levels, as was the case with the illustrated hierarchically classified index. If we decide to do this, we will be indexing the subject on several levels.

Depth of Index

The average number of index entries per document in a particular index is a measure of the depth of the index. The minimum depth of an index is one index entry per document and this might be the filing point of the document by subject or by author. The average depth of most printed alphabetic subject indexes is between two and five subject index entries plus the necessary author index entries. The average depth of a keyword-in-context index is about five subject entries. Coordinate indexes are usually of greater depth. Ten or more index units per document in a coordinate index are not uncommon.

Completeness of Collection Covered by the Index

This variable is, of course, independent of the type of index. It is mentioned here to bring out what probably is an obvious point to the reader but one that nevertheless bears consideration. If the collection that is to be indexed lacks many important documents in its subject area, then even an index which yields most relevant documents included in it may be inadequate because some of the important documents are not in the collection.

Form of Index, Mechanism of Preparation, and Searching

The different types of indexes can be on cards, in book form, on magnetic tape, or on film. The cards may be unpunched and unlined, index cards of various sizes, edge-notched punched cards, internally punched tabulating cards, or optical coincidence cards. The type of index will dictate to some extent its method of preparation and searching. The principal preparation options are to write by hand, to type, or to keypunch the index units. Searching is done either manually or by machine.

Index variables for 175 operating indexing systems are described in a recent publication issued by the National Science Foundation.[4] We will again refer to this publication when we discuss coordinate indexes.

INDEX EVALUATION

We are concerned with the evaluation of indexes so that we can determine how good a particular index is, or, if we are in the planning stage of an index, how good one index is likely to be in comparison with another. A number of factors can make an index good or bad. The documents that are included or excluded, respectively; the ease of getting at relevant documents when using the index; the cost of preparing and searching the index. These are some, but not all of the factors. To complicate things, a bad index may be best under some circumstances. For example, the least expensive index would be best for a collection that is not going to be used if the contents of the collection do not warrant its use. Under these circumstances an ideally bad index, the absence of the index, is least expensive and therefore best. The state of the art of index evaluation is also bad but not hopeless. There are a few guidelines and measuring sticks that we can use but it must be remembered that because of subjective factors that will be discussed subsequently, these measuring sticks lack the precision of instruments that are used by the physical scientist in his laboratory. We will discuss the evaluation of indexes in terms of typical search results, search time, and over-all cost of preparing and searching an index.

Measurement of Search Results

Let us again take the search results of our United States junior college architecture search to illustrate the measures for characterizing

	Retrieved	Nonretrieved	
Relevant	a	b	$a + b$
Nonrelevant	c	d	$c + d$
Total collection	$a + c$	$b + d$	$a + b + c + d$

Figure 2-4. Characterization of search results.

search results. We selected eight potentially relevant documents out of an estimated 10,000 documents that were included in this one volume of the index. Three of the eight potentially relevant documents turned out to be nonrelevant upon examination, leaving us five relevant documents. We will make an assumption that there are two and only two additional relevant documents in this volume of the index that we failed to select. The documents in the index can now be categorized into four groups and the number of documents in each group can be given. (It is usually very difficult or at least time consuming to determine what relevant documents are missed in a search and this is one of the difficulties in index evaluation.)

a. Relevant documents retrieved   5 documents
b. Relevant documents not retrieved   2 documents
c. Nonrelevant documents retrieved   3 documents
d. Nonrelevant documents not retrieved   9990 documents

Every search result can be characterized in terms of these four groups of documents which are identified by the letters "a" through "d." These four groups of documents will now be presented as a two-by-two contingency table, Figure 2-4.

The search results are usually expressed in terms of recall ratio and precision ratio and these are the measures that we will describe. Recall ratio is the ratio of relevant documents retrieved over total number of relevant documents in the index and multiplied by 100. Expressed in our notation: $a/(a + b) \times 100$. Precision ratio is the ratio of relevant documents retrieved over total number of documents retrieved in that search and multiplied by 100. Expressed in our notation this becomes $a/(a + c) \times 100$. For our search results, the recall ratio and the precision ratios are:

$$\text{Recall} = \frac{5}{5 + 2} \times 100 = 71\%$$

$$\text{Precision ratio} = \frac{5}{5 + 3} \times 100 = 62\%$$

Even though recall and precision ratios have been expressed as numbers, the quantitative nature of this measurement is deceptive. This is because judgment of relevance is a highly subjective matter, as has been determined in a number of studies. Such studies have shown that relevance judgment is not consistent even when done by the same individual at different times. The judgment will be influenced by the number of documents that need to be judged, the order in which these documents have been presented, and perhaps even what the judge had for breakfast that day.[5] Nevertheless, the recall ratio and precision ratios give a rough measure of index performance if this is measured on a number of representative searches and if we realize that it may contain a large margin of error. The next question to answer is, what is a satisfactory recall and precision ratio for an index? Once again the answer is less than satisfactory—it depends. A relatively high recall ratio, say 80% recall, may be specified if most of the documents on a topic are needed in the typical search. If, on the other hand, the searches are mostly a "few good articles on a subject," then a lower recall ratio may be quite satisfactory. The precision ratio is a measure of the index's success in screening out nonrelevant documents. This is more important for larger collections than we are likely to have in a researcher's personal document collection. In an index to 2000 documents where the average number of selected relevant documents may be 10 documents, a precision ratio of, say, 33% would not cause any particular problem. It is relatively easy to separate 10 out of 30 nonrelevant documents and the task of doing so is likely to be considerably less expensive than the task of preventing the selection of nonrelevant documents in the first place. On the other hand, in an index to a much larger collection with an average search result of 50 relevant documents, the screening of 50 out of 150 documents may be more of a problem and one that might be reduced through index design. Thus, the more important criterion for small indexes is the recall ratio. How high the average recall should be is a decision that the individual indexer must make based on his actual or anticipated search requirements. He must remember that close to 100% recall is rarely achieved and that the higher the recall the higher the indexing cost is likely to be.

Search Time

The amount of time that it takes to get the relevant documents for the average question is another measure of the efficiency of an index. This time consists of the combined time for the steps depicted in Figure 2-1 beginning with the translation of the search into the language of the index through the screening of potentially relevant documents step.

The average time of typical searches needs to be taken since some searches take very little time and others do not. When we measure average search time, we disregard adequacy of search results though these two factors are related. The adequacy of search results are considered in the recall and precision ratio measurements. In some cases, part of or even the entire search may be delegated to a research assistant or a secretary. This will affect the cost of the search, a topic that will be discussed next.

Over-all Cost of Index

The over-all cost of an index consists of the cost of design, preparation, and use of the index. The cost can also be divided into professional and clerical manpower, material, equipment, and the overhead required. Few precise figures are as yet available on indexing.[6] Cost figures available for particular indexing systems will be reported in the chapters on the types of indexes. We will make some general comments at this point on the cost, or more precisely on the economics of indexes. When an index is first prepared, almost all of the cost will be input cost—the cost of indexing. Until a large number of potentially useful documents is included in the index, almost all of the cost will be input cost. Even when the index is used on a regular basis, chances are that the input cost will be considerably higher than the output (searching) cost. Another generalization can be made about indexing which is usually true: there is an inverse ratio between input cost and output cost. To put this differently, the more it costs us to index documents, the less it will cost us to retrieve these documents. The implication of these points is that we should attempt to spread the costs in such a way that there is a reasonable balance between input and output costs. We should accept a reasonable search time per typical search since by doing so we are likely to save on indexing costs which are apt to represent the major costs of the index. A reasonable search time for the size of the document collection that we are talking about might be 5 to 20 minutes.

One of the major costs in the preparation of indexes is the preparation and use of the index vocabulary. This topic will be discussed in the next chapter.

REFERENCES

1. The process of searching an index has been of interest to librarians for many years. The process is quite complex and as yet incompletely understood. The

flowchart is thus an oversimplification. The reader is directed to the following references for a fuller discussion of the index searching process: Taylor, R. S., "The Process of Asking Questions," *American Documentation*, 13:391–396 (1962); Voress, H. E., "Searching Techniques in the Literature of the Sciences," *College and Research Libraries*, 24:209–212 (1963).

2. For our purpose, the basic unit in the question or subject heading may be a single word of a phrase. If a single word is dependent for its meaning upon another word in the question or subject heading, then this combination of words is considered as the basic unit.

3. For a fuller discussion of search logic, the reader is referred to Kent, A., *Textbook on Mechanized Information Retrieval*, 2nd ed. New York: Interscience, 1966, pp. 167–178.

4. National Science Foundation, *Nonconventional Scientific and Technical Information System in Current Use*, Number 4, National Science Foundations, December 1966.

5. The most extensive study on this subject was performed by Cuadra and Katter. The major conclusions of their study are that relevance judgment can be influenced by the skill and attitude of the particular judges, the documents and document sets used, the particular information requirement, the instructions and setting in which the judgment takes place, and the type of rating scale or other medium used to express the judgments. This study is summarized in the following reference: Cuadra, C. A. and Katter, R. V., "The Relevance of Relevance Judgment," *Proceedings of the Annual Meeting of the American Documentation Institute*, Volume 4, 1967, pp. 95–99.

6. Reasons why little cost information is available for information retrieval systems and a fuller discussion of the economics of such system are given in the following article. Batten, W. E., "The Economics of Information Retrieval," *Library Journal*, 92:974–975 (March 1, 1967).

Chapter Three

Controlled Index Vocabularies

In the previous chapter, control of indexing vocabulary was considered as an important index variable. The point was made that vocabulary control is a relative rather than an absolute matter. A controlled vocabulary in terms of a fixed or frozen vocabulary for an index to a changing subject would be an absurdity. Control of vocabulary refers to the use of existing or established index units, when this is possible, and to the controlled addition of new indexing units when necessary. The use of an index with a controlled vocabulary offers an advantage but does this at a cost. The advantage is the likelihood of higher recall ratios (the retrieval of a larger portion of the relevant documents) in searching the index. The disadvantage is the higher cost of indexing. And this may be too high a cost to pay for an index to a researcher's document collection. There are actually two incremental expenses involved: the cost of preparing the controlled vocabulary and the cost of using as well as up-dating the controlled vocabulary. While the latter cost may be justified, the former cost is usually not. To put it differently, if a controlled index vocabulary is available in your area of subject interest, consider the use of this vocabulary; if no such index vocabulary is available, do not attempt to generate your own.

In this chapter, reasons for considering the use of a controlled vocabulary are considered first. Then techniques for preparing and using a controlled vocabulary are discussed. The chapter concludes with a list of references to controlled vocabularies in selected subject areas.

Let us begin with the question, "Why is a controlled vocabulary desirable in an indexing system?" The meaning of a word—the relationship of the sign and the object designated—is usually not a one-to-one relationship. And this presents a problem in the preparation and searching of indexes. At the risk of exhausting the reader's patience with the subject of the architecture of junior colleges, we will again use this example. There are at least two other phrases that have the same meaning as the phrase "junior colleges" and these are "community colleges" and "two-year colleges." Unless a rule is made to use one of these three phrases whenever the topic junior colleges is to be indexed, there is the danger that it will be indexed under "junior colleges" part of the time and under the other two phrases the rest of the time. This would result in only partial retrieval of documents on junior colleges when searching the heading "junior colleges." The solution to this problem is simple and probably self-evident to the reader: choose one phrase as the index heading and make cross-references to that chosen phrase. If "junior colleges" becomes the chosen phrase, then the following "*see*" references are made in the index:

Community colleges
  See Junior colleges
Two-year colleges
  See Junior colleges

The preparation of "*see*" references for synonyms is one of the techniques used in vocabulary control. But this step does not solve all of the vocabulary problems. There is also the problem of words that have similar but not the same meaning—near synonyms. In an index to documents in the field of marketing there may be documents dealing with cash purchases and documents dealing with credit purchases, and perhaps documents dealing with both forms of purchases. These are related but not the same concepts and the difference might have to be brought out in an index in which there are many documents on purchasing. The difference can be indicated by having two indexing units labelled "cash purchases" and "credit purchases," respectively. The relationship between these two index units is indicated by means of the following two "*see also*" references:

Cash purchases
  See also Credit purchases
Credit purchases
  See also Cash purchases

In an index which includes few documents on purchasing and in which this is a relatively unimportant topic, the two near synonyms can be treated as synonyms and grouped under the more generic heading "Purchases." The following cross-reference should then be provided to make this decision clear:

Credit purchases
   See Purchases
Cash purchases
   See Purchases

Another problem is that of homonyms, words with more than one meaning. When we use the word "bond," do we mean an atomic bond, or a physical bond supplied by an adhesive, or a bond that is posted to keep a person out of jail, or a bond that gives a share in the ownership of a corporation? The word "bond" could have these as well as other meanings. In writing or conversation, meaning is supplied by context. This also needs to be added in indexing to avoid ambiguity. Context is provided by a parenthetical word or phrase following the index heading. For example, the index heading for chemical bond might be "Bond (chemical)," for physical bond "Bond (physical)," for legal bond, "Bond (legal)," for financial bond, "Bond (financial)," and so on. Notice that the same word can appear in an index several times with different parenthetical statements.

Still another problem is the problem of generics which was touched upon in the last chapter in the discussion on levels of indexing. The same subject can be indexed and therefore searched at different levels of specificity as was shown in the North America, Florida, Leon County, Tallahassee example. A partial solution to this problem is to instruct the indexer to index as specifically as the subject permits. This does not solve the entire problem for the searcher since he may have to search on different levels of specificity. If all of the documents on Florida are wanted, one cannot search only under "Florida" since some documents will be on parts of Florida, perhaps Leon County, and will therefore have to be searched under the generic term "Florida" and the specific terms for parts of Florida. In one type of index, the hierarchically classified index, the more generic (broader) concepts are included in the specific (narrower) concepts as was illustrated in the last chapter. For the other indexes, the specific-generic relationships can be spelled out either by a separate listing of specific-generic "word families" or by cross-references. Examples of both types of displays are given in Figures 3-1 and 3-2. These displays of generic-specific relationships among indexing terms are intended to assist the searcher in his selection of indexing terms.

Materials
  .
  .
  Metals
  .
  .
  Plastics
    Thermoplastics
      Acetal plastics
      Acrylic plastics
      .
      .
      Vinyl plastics
        .
        .
        Polyvinyl alcohol
        Polyvinyl chloride
  .
  .
  Wood

Figure 3-1. Excerpt of display of specific-generic relationship among indexing terms—classified (hierarchical) arrangement of indexing terms.

In a coordinate index in which phrases are split into single word headings, there may also be a problem of difference of meanings of phrases with different word orders. A commonly used, though hardly realistic, example of this is the phrase "Venetian blind." If this phrase were to be indexed in a coordinate index by the words "Venetian" and "blind," and if a searcher were to look in this index for documents

Plastics
  See also
    Materials (BT)
    Acetal plastics (NT)
    Acrylic plastics (NT)
    Polyvinyl alcohol (NT)
    Polyvinyl chloride (NT)
    Thermoplastics (NT)
    Vinyl plastics (NT)
Vinyl plastics
  See also
    Materials (BT)
    Plastics (BT)
    Thermoplastics (BT)
    Polyvinyl alcohol (NT)
    Polyvinyl chloride (NT)

Figure 3-2. Excerpt of display of specific-generic relationships among indexing terms listing of broader terms (BT) and narrower terms (NT) under each indexing term.

on sightless people in the city of Venice (and here the example becomes unrealistic), he might get a document on Venetian blinds. A somewhat more realistic example is the splitting up of the phrase "school library," the library in a school, into "school" and "library" and obtaining documents on library schools (schools for educating librarians) when searching under these two words. This type of problem can be avoided by not splitting the potentially troublesome phrase into its constituent parts.

A subject authority list is a device for reducing vocabulary problems by means that we have mentioned: *"see"* and *"see also"* cross references, parenthetical statements, and indication of generic-specific relationships. An excerpt of a subject authority list, often called a thesaurus, is given in Figure 3-3. In this list, "Aeronautics" was selected as an index unit and "Aviation" as a synonym for aeronautics. This is recorded as an index decision by the cross-reference "Aviation *See* Aeronautics." The *"Refer from* Aviation" notation is a record that a decision has been made to include "Aviation" under "Aeronautics." The *"see also"* references indicate related terms. Three types of related terms are listed: narrower (more specific) terms than Aeronautics and these are all the terms followed by a designation (NT); broader (more generic) terms than Aeronautics and this is the term followed by the designation (BT); terms that are neither related specifically nor generically but related in another, undefined way and this is the term followed by the designation (RT). The index unit "Drones (Pilotless Planes)" is an example of an index term that is defined by a qualifying phrase.

The subject authority list is used by both the indexer and the searcher to translate the indexable information into index units. The indexer takes each unit of indexable information and looks it up in the subject authority list. The unit of indexable information may be identical to the established index unit or it may lead to an established index unit by means of a cross-reference. These two examples may be illustrated by the terms aeronautics and aviation, respectively. In both cases, an indexing decision has already been made to use "Aeronautics" and this is recorded in the subject authority list. If the unit of indexable information to be translated were to be "dirigibles" (Blimp), a term not as yet recorded in the index, then the indexer would either refer "dirigible (Blimp)" to "Balloons" by means of a *"see"* cross-reference or establish a new index unit "Dirigibles (Blimp)" and connect this new index unit to related index units, such as "Aeronautics."

> "Dirigibles (Blimp)"
> Aeronautics (BT)
> Aeronautics
> Dirigibles (Blimp) (NT)

AERONAUTICS
  See also
    Aerospace Industries and Sciences (for inclusion) (BT)
    Air-cushion Vehicles (NT)
    Airlines (NT)
    Airplanes (NT)
    Airports (NT)
    Airships (NT)
    Astronautics (RT)
    Balloons (NT)
    Drones (Pilotless Planes) (NT)
    Gliders (NT)
    Helicopters (NT)
    Missiles (NT)
    Parachutes and Parachute Jumping (NT)
    Unidentified Flying Objects (NT)
    Wind Tunnels **(NT)**
  Refer from
    Aviation
.
.
.

Aviation
  See
    Aeronautics

Figure 3-3. Excerpt from *The New York Times.* Thesaurus of Descriptors." A guide for organizing, cataloguing, indexing, and searching collections of information on current events. *New York Times,* 1968.

Now to the searcher's use of the subject authority list. The searcher translates his question into the language of the index as a preliminary step to searching the index. This is done with the help of the subject authority list. Each component of the search question is checked in the authority list to locate established index (search) units. If an index unit corresponding to a search question unit cannot be located, the searcher has a problem. He will have to reformulate his question to correspond with the available index vocabulary if this is possible, or give up on the use of the index (at least for this one question) if this is not possible.

We are including a brief description of how a subject authority list is prepared. This topic is dealt with in greater detail in references cited by Gaster.[1] The preparation of a subject authority list begins with a compilation of word lists from which potential index terms will be selected. Word lists to be scanned might include specialized dictionaries and glossaries, textbooks, indexes to periodical articles, and representative documents from the collection that is to be indexed. Words and phrases are selected from one or more of these word lists and the selected words and phrases represent the raw list of terms that will be refined into the subject authority list. The unrefined word list may consist of several hundred terms if a subject authority list is to be prepared for a narrow subject or as many as 50,000 terms if it is for a broad subject such as engineering.[2] Even several hundred words and phrases are very difficult to compare with each other unless the words and phrases are divided into smaller groups. If the subject of the word list is in the area of science and technology, the grouping might be by terms dealing with processes, products, properties, materials, equipment, and abstract concepts, respectively. An "other" category is usually provided for terms that do not fit anywhere else. If this first grouping yields about 100 or fewer terms in the largest group, the analysis of the individual terms can be started. Usually, further subdivision is required to have manageable groups of terms. Each of the groups that contains more than 100 or so terms is further subdivided and if the "other" group is too large, it may yield one or more meaningful subject groupings. An example of subgroupings of terms is the subdivision of properties terms into terms dealing with chemical properties, physical properties, biological properties, and other properties. The next step in the analysis of terms that are now in small groups can then be started. This analysis consists of combining singular and plural forms of nouns, and combining different word forms. For example, the terms analysis, analyses, analyzed, analyzing may all be combined into the noun form, analysis. Synonyms are also combined, and near synonyms are either combined or related to each other, homonyms are differentiated by means of parenthetical statements and specific-generic relationships and other relationships among indexing terms are indicated. This procedure is used for the terms in each of the subject groupings. The grouping is an artificial device for facilitating the analysis of the raw list of terms. Once the index units have been established and relationships among indexing units within each group have been recorded, relationships among indexing units in the different groupings are also identified and recorded. When all of these steps have been completed, the subject authority list (or at least the first, and usually tentative edition) is produced. The arrangement of the list is alphabetic by index terms and cross-references. In some cases the alphabetic list is supplemented by an arrangement of index terms by word families—the generic-specific arrangement. The preface of the subject authority list typically states how the list is to be used by the searcher and indexer and how it is to be revised. The list is usually out-of-date as soon as it is ready to use since new documents indexed with the aid of a subject authority list require revision of the list.

To summarize:

1. The preparation of a subject authority list especially for an index to a researcher's document collection is not recommended because it is a very time-consuming process.

2. The use of an existing subject authority list prepared for another index, if one is available in the subject of interest to the researcher, is likely to result in more consistent indexing. More consistent indexing is likely to yield a larger proportion of relevant documents in searching the index (higher recall), but this is accomplished at a higher over-all cost of the index. The higher indexing cost comes from the need to translate the indexable information into the language of the index and from the need for revising the subject authority list as new indexing decisions have to be made.

3. The subject authority list must be updated when indexable information cannot be translated into the language of the index. This is done by either expanding the scope of an existing index unit to include the meaning of the indexable information or by establishing a new indexing unit. In both cases the necessary cross-references and other relationships need to be recorded for the new or revised index units. ·

REFERENCES

1. Gaster, K., "Thesaurus Construction and Use. A Selective Bibliography Based on Material in Aslib Library in July 1967," *Aslib Proceedings,* **19**:310–317 (1967).
2. For example, the Engineers Joint Council thesaurus of engineering terms listed under index vocabularies in science and technology is based on a preliminary list of over 87,000 terms.

LIST OF INDEX VOCABULARIES OF POTENTIAL USE FOR PERSONAL DOCUMENTS COLLECTIONS

Humanities

Arts Index. New York: H. W. Wilson, 1929–
British Humanities Index. London: The Library Association, 1962–   .
The Music Index. Detroit, Michigan: Information Service, Inc., 1949–   . (List of subject headings published separately.)
Social Sciences and Humanities Index. New York: H. W. Wilson, 1916–   .

Science and Technology

American Chemical Society, Chemical Abstracts Service. *Chemical-Biological Activities World Guide*, 2nd ed. Columbus, Ohio: American Chemical Society, 1967.
Applied Science and Technology Index. New York: H. W. Wilson, 1913–   .
Engineers Joint Council, *Thesaurus of Engineering Terms and their Relations for Use in Vocabulary Control Indexing and Retrieving Engineering Information*. New York: The Council, 1964.
National Library of Medicine, *Medical Subject Headings*. Washington, D.C.: U.S. Department of Health, Education, and Welfare. (Part 2 of January issue of Index Medicus.)
U.S. Armed Forces Technical Information Agency, *Thesaurus of ASTIA Descriptors*, 2nd ed. Arlington, Virginia: U.S. Armed Forces Technical Information Agency, 1962.
U.S. Public Health Service. *Medical and Health Related Sciences Thesaurus*. Washington, D.C.: U.S. Public Health Service, 1963.

Social Sciences

Economic Abstracts. New York: New York University, 1953–56.
Historical Abstracts: Bibliography of the World's Periodical Literature. Santa Barbara, California: American Bibliographic Center, 1955–   .
International Affairs. Universal Reference System, Political Science, Government and Public Policy Series. Princeton, New Jersey: Princeton Research Publishing, 1965–   .

Additional lists of index vocabularies are included in the following bibliographies:

National Federation of Science Abstracting and Indexing Services, *A Guide to the World's Abstracting and Indexing Services in Science and Technology*. Washington, D.C.: U.S. Public Health Service, 1963.
Special Libraries Association, *Guide to the SLA Loan Collection of Classification Schemes and Subject Heading Lists on Deposit at Western Reserve University as of March 20, 1961*, 5th ed. New York: SLA Special Classification Committee, 1961.
U.S. Library of Congress Catalog, *Books: Subject*. Washington, D.C.: Library of Congress, 1950–   . (Index vocabularies are listed under "Subject headings.")

Chapter Four

Conventional Indexes

Three conventional indexes, the alphabetic subject index, the hierarchically classified index, and the alphabetico-classified index, will be discussed in this chapter. Figure 4-1 illustrates a typical index heading for each of the three indexes.

The individual index headings are arranged alphabetically in the alphabetic subject index and the alphabetico-classified index and numerically in the illustrated hierarchically classified index. As has been pointed out in the first two chapters, each type of index can be prepared with certain options. These include the amount of information given in the index entry about the indexed document, the depth of the index (the average number of index entries per document), and the physical form of the index. There are also options that apply to some but not all of the types of indexes, and these options will be discussed when the individual indexes are described.

Before we begin the discussion of the individual conventional indexes, let us review the differences between conventional and coordinate indexes. In the conventional indexes, the access point for each index heading is selected at the time of indexing. The access point is usually modified with a word or a phrase to form the index heading. Conventional indexes can only be searched under access points selected at the

Aluminum
546.673
Chemistry—Inorganic—
Metallic elements—Aluminum

Alphabetic subject index
Hierarchically classified
Alphabetico-classified

Figure 4-1. Index heading for the subject "Aluminum" in three conventional indexes.

time of the indexing and with index headings that consist of combinations of words also selected and combined at the time of indexing. In coordinate indexes, access points are also chosen at the time of indexing. However, and this is the principal difference between conventional and coordinate indexes, coordinate indexes can either be searched by access points chosen at the time of indexing or by any logical combination of such access points.

There is another difference between conventional and coordinate indexes that is derived from this difference. For the same depth of index, a larger number of index units must be prepared for a conventional index than for a coordinate index. This is because all of the index headings have to be prepared as separate physical units at the time of indexing for conventional indexes, while for coordinate indexes only the building blocks (the access points) of index headings need to be prepared and made into physical units. Thus conventional indexes require more clerical manpower than coordinate indexes of the same depth. One can also argue that conventional indexes require more intellectual effort than coordinate indexes that are equivalent in depth since the indexer of the conventional index has to anticipate and provide for various combinations of topics that form the index heading at the time of indexing.

ALPHABETIC SUBJECT INDEX

The word or phrase that makes up the index heading in an alphabetic subject index is filed alphabetically in a single alphabetic sequence. There is little or no inversion of phrase headings from their natural language sequence. For example, the phrase heading "Chemical engineer" would be filed under "Chemical engineer," its natural language order, rather than under "Engineer, chemical," the inverted form of the phrase. The alphabetic subject index is familiar to researchers since they have been subjected to it when using library card catalogs, the "Yellow Pages" of telephone directories (incorrectly called classified sections of telephone directories), and most indexes to books and periodicals. And this familiarity is an advantage both in the preparation and use of such an index. Another advantage is that the individual index headings in this index can be as specific as desired. Specificity is achieved by using a specific access point and, when necessary, modifying this access point with a word or phrase to make the index heading even more specific. An example will illustrate. In an index to chemical documents, the name of a specific chemical may be considered to be a specific access point. If, however, there are a number of documents in the index that deal with the chemical in question, the index heading can be made more specific by adding to the name of the chemical what is being said about it in the indexed document—its method of preparation, its cost, its reactions, its properties, or whatever. Still another advantage of this index is that it does not have a rigid or fixed structure. This is not an unmixed blessing as we shall see later on, but for now let us point to the advantage of this flexibility. One does not need a complete list, nor any list for that matter, of index headings before starting to index with an alphabetic subject index. One can make up individual index headings as one goes along with the indexing. (This is not to say that this is the recommended procedure. Consideration should be given to the use of an established list of index headings with cross-references if such a list is available, as was pointed out in the previous chapter.) Such an index is also hospitable to new subjects that may need to be included as well as to changes in subject terminology. This, of course, is a distinct advantage in rapidly changing fields. Index headings for new subjects or changes in terminology can be made in the index with relative ease—by defining potentially ambiguous new terms and by making necessary cross-references to existing index headings.

There are also negative aspects to this type of index. The permissiveness in the selection of index headings can cause search problems. If the singular form of a noun is used part of the time as an access point and the plural form of the noun is used as an access point the rest of the time, information on the same subject is going to be dispersed in the index. The same problem will occur if the noun, verb, adjective, or other word forms are used interchangeably as access point for the same subject. Also, there is the problem of expressing the same subject in different phrase forms. An example would be to have an index heading "Structure of buildings" and another index heading in the same index "Building structure." Information on the same subject would also be dispersed thereby and would tend to make search results incomplete. Perhaps the most serious criticism of the alphabetic subject index is that it tends to disperse related information even if care is taken to avoid the word and phrase form problem. This is because the arrangement of the index heading is by order of the letters in the alphabet rather than by subject. Related topics are dispersed throughout the index. If an index were to list index headings for various types of engineers in their uninverted (natural language) form and if one needed to conduct a search for all types of engineers, one would have to look under the index headings "Aeronautical engineer," "Chemical engineer," "Civil engineer," "Electrical engineer," "Mechanical engineer," and perhaps even under the names of other types of engineers, and under "Engineers" for documents that are on engineers in general. This presents a problem in conducting generic searches. A list of specific subject headings that make up the generic topic must first be compiled, which is not always an easy task. In fact, it is easy to leave out specific subject-headings when making such a list. If we had *"see also"* cross-references from the generic to specific topics, this would help but it is impossible to make *"see also"* cross-references for all generic searches. There are just too many generic searches that *might* be conducted.

Coordinate searches are also difficult to conduct in an alphabetic subject index. By this we mean searches that require the coordination or combination of components of different index headings in an alphabetic subject index. An example will be given. Let us assume we have the following two index headings in an alphabetic subject index:

Automotive fuels, production costs
Jet fuels, production costs

Let us further assume that there are no access points in this index under either "Fuels" or "Production costs." A search for production costs of fuels is a coordinate search which would be very difficult to conduct in this index. In order to get around this problem, attempts are made to prepare index headings that are made up of the combination of words likely to be searched. This is usually not completely successful since not all likely word combinations can be predicted and even if they could be predicted the cost of providing them in the index would be too high.

If either generic or coordinate searches are anticipated as typical types of searches rather than exceptional types of searches, then an index other than an alphabetic subject index should be considered.

HIERARCHICALLY CLASSIFIED INDEX

In a hierarchically classified index, the field of knowledge covered by the index (and this may be all of knowledge in a general index) is arranged in a hierarchy which is a grouping of related topics beginning with the most general (generic) topic and going to the more specific topics in two or more steps. The specific topic is always included in the more generic topics. In such an index, the hierarchy must be established before the indexing can be started since every topic has a predetermined and fixed location in the hierarchy. Room for growth and expansion of topics is allowed in the hierarchy, again in predetermined and fixed locations. In indexing, documents or portions thereof are assigned to individual locations within the hierarchy. These locations are identified by a code, sometimes called a notation, which stands for the topic. This code represents the hierarchical structure of each subject. The reader is familiar with a hierarchically classified index through his use of the Dewey Decimal or Library of Congress classification system. Both of these systems are used in libraries for the physical arrangement of books on the shelves. Since a book can only be shelved in one place, only one subject code is assigned to each book. The one subject assignment per document is not an inherent limitation of classified indexes. Two or more hierarchically classified subject index entries can be assigned to each document. Bolles describes a hierarchically classified index that he designed for the document collection in his office.[1] An extract of the index which Bolles derived from the Dewey Decimal system is given in Figure 4-2.

The illustrated example shows a hierarchy of six levels. Notice that the most specific subject (characterized at the third decimal point) always includes every one of the more generic subjects that are characterized by a number to the left of the number standing for the most specific subject.

One of the weaknesses of the alphabetic subject index is a strength of the hierarchically classified index. Generic searches are relatively easy to conduct if the proper hierarchy has been chosen for this particular search (more about this later). Specific searches, on the other hand, may not be as easy to conduct in a hierarchically classified index since the index headings are usually not as specific as with an alphabetic subject index. Coordinate searches are also difficult to conduct with such an index. The numbers, letters, or combination of numbers and letters that represent the index heading in the hierarchically classified index are shorter than their natural language equivalent. This shorthand notation saves writing time as well as space. But this is only part of the story since the natural language has to be translated into the notation of the index, both when indexing with this index and when searching the index. A separate alphabetic index is required to translate the natural language into the index notation. It is a requirement since no one (or

600	Economics and management
630	Economic evaluation
633	Manufacturing cost estimation
633.1	Direct costs
633.11	Chemicals and materials
633.12	Labor and supervision
633.13	Utilities
633.131	Steam
633.132	Water
633.133	Electricity
633.134	Fuels
633.135	Compressed air
633.14	Maintenance and materials
633.15	Royalties
633.16	Laboratory costs
633.17	Miscellaneous direct costs (supplies, etc.)
633.2	Indirect costs
633.21	Taxes
633.22	Insurance
633.23	Depreciation
633.24	Administration and overhead
633.25	Capital charges

Figure 4-2. Except of hierarchically classified index in the field of chemical engineering.

at least very few people) is going to remember a long list of notations that stand for the index headings in natural language. And this required translation step takes time and introduces an additional source of error into the system. Another disadvantage of the hierarchically classified index is the rigid and often arbitrary structure of the system. The designer of the system needs not only to provide space for all existing subjects in a given area (which is difficult) but he must also predict and provide spaces for future expansion of the subject included in the index (which is impossible). Also, it is difficult if not impossible to provide for all combinations and relationships among subjects in what is a two-dimensional array. Last but not least, the established hierarchy may not be useful for the organization of subjects that are of interest to an individual researcher. Thus if a hierarchy places the topic "Dogs" in the taxonomic order of the animal kingdom and you are interested in dogs as pets, or as carriers of rabies, or as drivers of Eskimo sleds, or as food eaten by Indians, you would find the animal kingdom taxonomy less than satisfactory.

Hierarchically classified indexes may be of potential use for researchers' document collections if an adequate index of this type is in existence and if the generic search is the typical rather than the exceptional type of search. Unless these two conditions apply, another type of index should be considered.

ALPHABETICO-CLASSIFIED INDEX

An alphabetico-classified index is a hybrid between an alphabetic subject index and a hierarchically classified index. In this type of index, the specific topic is the last listed element of the index heading and this specific topic is always preceded by at least one more generic representation of this topic. In the alphabetico-classified index illustrated in Figure 4-1, the specific topic "Aluminum" is preceded by three more generic characterizations of this topic: "Metallic elements," "Inorganic," and "Chemistry." The index heading is filed alphabetically under its access point and this gives the alphabetico-classified index its alphabetic feature. The grouping of the specific topic under the more generic topic or topics is the classified aspect of the index. The alphabetic arrangement of the index headings (which are in natural language rather than in coded form) eliminates the need for a separate alphabetic index that is required in the hierarchically classified index. The arrangement of the index heading under a broad subject makes this a more suitable index for conducting generic searches than the alphabetic subject index. Despite these real advantages, the alphabetico-classified index is not in common use in the United States. This is probably because the index is not easy to either prepare or use. It is difficult for both the indexer and the searcher to determine how, and how extensively, a subject should be divided. This is also a problem of the hierarchically classified index but it is more firmly established and at least in the case of the Dewey Decimal, the Universal Decimal, and the Library of Congress systems, these indexes are used so extensively that groups of individuals are charged with the task of improving and updating them. As with the other two conventional indexes, coordinate searches are difficult to conduct in an alphabetico-classified index.

While an alphabetico-classified index to a researcher's document collection might not be the most desirable index to use for reasons stated above, segments of an alphabetic subject index might be improved by incorporating a classified structure for topics that are likely to be searched generically. This might be done by phrase inversion or by including a hierarchical structure for selected topics.

CONCLUSION

To find out which of the advantages and disadvantages of the conventional indexes as well as of the coordinate indexes are important, the individual researcher must first know his indexing needs in terms of the characteristics of these indexes. Guidelines for doing this will be discussed in a later chapter. No time figures for preparing these indexes have been given since the preparation time depends on a number of factors that are likely to be different in different situations. The factors include the depth of the index, whether or not vocabulary control is used, how much information about the indexed document accompanies the index heading, and the indexer's typing skill. The bulk of the indexing time is required for the process of becoming familiar with the document. If the document is going to be read for other purposes as well, then the entire reading cost should probably not be charged to the indexing operation. Once the document has been read, preparation of index entries will take anywhere from 2 to 20 minutes or more per document. A more precise figure can be obtained by timing oneself for the indexing of a sample of documents, remembering that greater speed will be achieved with practice. Each of these conventional indexes can be prepared in either book or card form. No equipment other than a typewriter is required for preparing the conventional indexes. Equipment for filing the index entries and the documents is discussed in a later chapter.

REFERENCES

1. Bolles, W. L., "Decimal Classification System for Chemical Engineering." *Petroleum Refiner*, **28**(5):140–148 (May 1949).

The following books and journal article include discussions of conventional indexes.

Bernier, C. L., "Subject-Index Production." *Library Trends*, **16**:388–397 (January 1968).

Coates, E. J., *Subject Catalogues: Headings and Structure*. London: The Library Association, 1960.

Foskett, D. J., *Classification and Indexing in the Social Sciences*. London: Butterworths, 1963.

Sharp, J. R., *Some Fundamentals of Information Retrieval*. New York: London House and Maxwell, 1965.

Vickery, B. C., *Classification and Indexing in Science*, 2nd ed. London: Butterworths, 1959.

Chapter Five

Coordinate Indexes

Coordinate indexes have not been on the scene for too many years but are now getting a lot of attention. A gentleman by the name of Taylor is credited as being the first recorded user of a coordinate index and in 1915 he was rewarded a U.S. patent for the disclosure of his scheme.[1] Mr. Taylor was a birdwatcher and he found existing tools for bird identification inadequate. By the time he could identify the bird from its characteristic plumage, size, crest, color, or stance with the aid of a conventional index, the bird would disappear, frightened no doubt by the noise made when pages of the index were hurriedly turned. Mr. Taylor's invention overcame the problems of the prior art. He prepared a small piece of cardboard (or other writing surface) upon which were recorded the names of the birds to be identified. A similar writing surface of the same size was used for recording identifying characteristics of the birds. Holes were made on each of these cards so that when the card of identifying characteristic was superimposed on the card for the birds, the name of the bird that had the particular characteristic would show through. If, for example, we had a card for birds with a crest, the names cardinal, blue jay, and all other birds with this characteristic could be read on the base card. In identifying a particular bird, cards for as many of its characteristics as could be assembled in a hurry were superimposed on the base (name of birds) card. In theory, at least, the name of the bird that could be seen through the superimposed cards represented the name of the bird to be identified. If we were to replace the name of the birds card with a card that stands for document serial numbers and replace the characteristics of birds cards with cards that characterize subjects of documents, we would have a coordinate index similar to the optical coincidence index that will be described in this chapter. In both instances, sought objects are identified by matching, or coordinating, specified characteristics. During the past twenty years or so, a number of coordinate indexes have been in use. Coordinate indexes to 175 documents collections in the fields of science and technology (excluding indexes to personal document collections) are described in a National Science Foundation publication.[2] We will discuss in some detail three forms of coordinate indexes that are of potential use in the indexing of personal document collections: the Uniterm, optical coincidence, and edge-notched cards forms. But first we will introduce a small document collection that will be of assistance in describing the coordinate indexes.

Let us assume that we have a sample collection of six documents. The collection is indexed with an index vocabulary reproduced in Figure 5-1.

We will call the units of the index vocabulary descriptors, though they have also been called uniterms, keyterms, concepts, unit concepts, classiterms, aspects, and various other names. Notice that the descriptors are grouped under broad or generic topics, the underlined words or phrases. Some of these broad topics are also useful for conducting generic searches and we will therefore use the topics "Office," "Issues," and "Actions" as descriptors as well as the words or phrases listed under the broad topics. Since we will index under the corresponding generic descriptor whenever we index under the specific descriptor, our index is on two levels, the broad and specific levels. The six documents along with their descriptors are listed below.

Document 1. 1964 U.S. presidential vote analyzed by Republican votes for the Republican candidate and Democratic votes for the Democratic candidate.
Descriptors:

Office	Actions
U.S. Presidency	Votes
Democratic candidate	1964
Democrats	Republican candidate
	Republicans

Office
___
U.S. Presidency
People
___
Democratic candidates
Democrats
Females
Males
Negroes
Republican candidates
Republicans
Whites
Issues
___
Discrimination
Employment opportunities
Foreign policy
Gun control
Housing
Taxes
Actions
___
Speeches
Votes
Types or forms of documents
___
Opinion polls
Review
Dates
___
1964
March 1968
August 1968
1968

Figure 5-1. Index vocabulary for sample document collection.

Document 2. March 1968 opinion poll of Whites on Negro employment opportunities.
Descriptors:

Negroes	Employment opportunities
Whites	Opinion polls
Issues	March 1968

Document 3. June 1968 opinion poll of white males on U.S. foreign policy.
Descriptors:

Males	Foreign policy
Whites	Opinion polls
Issues	June 1968

Document 4. August 1968 opinion poll of white females on gun control.

Descriptors:

Females	Gun control
Whites	Opinion polls
Issues	August 1968

Document 5. Review of opinion polls on discrimination against Negroes in housing.

Descriptors:

Negroes	Housing
Issues	Opinion polls
Discrimination	Review

Document 6. Speeches made in 1968 by Democratic candidate for U.S. Presidency on foreign policy, gun control, and taxes.

Descriptors:

Office	Gun control
U.S. Presidency	Foreign policy
People	Actions
Democratic candidate	Speeches
Issues	1968

The indexed sample document collection is intended to serve several purposes: to introduce the concept of false drops, to discuss the use of roles and links as devices for reducing false drops, to review logical searches that can be done with coordinate indexes, and finally, to illustrate the use of the three forms of coordinate indexes that will be discussed.

False Drops, Links, and Roles

A false drop is a document selected in the course of an index search which is not on the topic of that particular search. It is thus an erroneously retrieved, unwanted, and nonrelevant document in a given search. If we were to search our sample index for documents on Republican votes for the Democratic candidate for the U.S. presidency in 1964 by looking for documents that are indexed under "Republicans," "Votes," "Democratic candidate," "U.S. Presidency," and "1964," we would be directed to Document 1. Document 1 would be a false drop for this search since it deals with Republicans voting for the Republican candidate for the U.S. presidency and the Democrats voting for the Democratic candidate for the U.S. presidency. The false drop occurred because we made a search for documents that shared specified descriptors (which Document 1 does) without also specifying that the descriptors had to be related to each other by other than the sometimes accidental relationship of being selected for the same document. This type of false drop can be reduced by not only listing descriptors for a document but by also indicating which descriptors are related to each other in a document. The device for indicating relationships among descriptors is called a link. Links are common symbols (letters or numbers) assigned to indicate relationships among descriptors in a document. If we used numbers as links in our example, Document 1 would have the following links:

Republicans	Democratic candidate	Actions
1-1	1-2	1-1,2
Republican candidate	Office	Votes
1-1	1-1,2	1-1,2
Democrats	U.S. Presidency	1964
1-2	1-1,2	1-1,2

The first number is the document number (1), the number or numbers following the hyphen are the links. Note that the descriptors U.S. Presidency, Office, Votes, Actions, and 1964 have both links 1 and 2 since they are related to both "Republican" and "Democratic" descriptors. A search of the index with links would be for documents that have not only the required descriptors but also the required descriptors with common links. In searching, we cannot specify the numeric value of the link since this is likely to differ from document to document. (In some documents, the link for related descriptors may be a "1," in others a "2" or a "3.") Instead we specify a common link—this could be a 1, or 2, or another number. If we had made our search for linked descriptors, Document 1 would not have been selected. In fact, we would not have selected any document because there aren't any on this subject in our collection. Should links be used in an index to a personal documents collection? Probably not. The use of links adds to the indexing cost. It takes longer to select descriptors and determine which descriptors should be linked to each other than to select descriptors only. Also, the mechanics of including links in an index, as exemplified by the addition of a symbol to the document number, adds to the cost of indexing. The use of links does not eliminate false drops but only reduces their occurrence. It is difficult to predict how many false drops to expect in a search since this depends on the size of the index vocabulary, the number of descriptors coordinated, the type of logical search that is being performed and, in the case of the index on edge-notched cards, the type of code used. Even a large percentage of false drops, say 100%, may not be a problem if the average search results in about 10 documents. It does not take much time to eliminate 5 false drops out of 10 documents in a search. If false drops do become a problem, other corrective action can be taken. One such action is to divide the potentially offending documents into two or more parts and treat these parts as separate documents. Thus Document 1 could become two documents, one dealing with Democrats voting for the Democratic candidate, and the second dealing with Republicans voting for the Republican candidate. This solution raises another potential problem since the separation of descriptors for one document makes it difficult to locate the original document when searching with descriptors that are in separate "documents." For example, if we were to separate Document 1 into Document 100 which deals with the Republican vote for the Republican candidate and into Document 101 which deals with the Democratic vote for the Democratic candidate, and if we searched for a document that compares the Democratic vote for the Democratic candidate and Republican vote for the Republican candidate, our original Document 1 would be difficult to retrieve even though it is on this subject. Another way of reducing the chance of false drops is to reduce the number of descriptors that are coordinate in searches by pre-coordinating descriptors into longer phrases. While this reduces the potential number of false drops, it also reduces one of the principal advantages of coordinate indexes, the ability of searching the index by combining or coordinating descriptors. As the number of words per phrase heading increases, the index units of the coordinate index will resemble more and more the index units of a conventional index and, as more information is included per descriptor, the possibility of and need for searching for combination of descriptors will be reduced correspondingly. This is, of course, a relative matter. Phrase headings are used as descriptors when components of the phrase are usually searched together or when the separation of the phrase heading into two or more descriptors is likely to cause false drop problems. In our index vocabulary, the phrase Republican candidate was used as a descriptor, partly because the two words are frequently used in combination, partly as a way of avoiding false drops.

False drops can also result for another reason, and this is illustrated by a search in our index for documents dealing with an opinion poll of Negroes' thinking about the employment opportunities of Whites. We conduct this search by coordinating descriptors "Opinion polls," "Negroes," "Employment opportunities," and "Whites," and retrieve Document 2 even though it is not on this subject. Links cannot be used to eliminate this type of false drop. These descriptors *are* related to each other but in a more subtle way than can be indicated with links. To avoid this type of false drop, another device called a role indicator or, simply, a role, needs to be used. Roles characterize the function performed or role played by a descriptor in a given document. In our search, a false drop would have been avoided for this search if we had assigned roles to the descriptors "Negroes" and "Whites." The roles could have been "Comments by" and "Commented upon," respectively. Roles have been used in coordinate indexes to collections in the field of science and technology. In chemistry, for example, roles can be used to characterize the function of a chemical in a reaction that is described in a document. The role can be assigned to signify the meanings reagent, intermediary, product, solvent, or catalyst, just to give some examples. Roles can be incorporated in a coordinate index in different ways. One way is to characterize the role by a letter or number which is added to the document number as either a prefix or a suffix. If the roles are indicated by a letter prefix in our index and if "Comments by" is characterized by the letter A and "Comments upon" by the letter B, then the two descriptions with role in Document 2 would appear in the index as

Whites	Negroes
A-2	B-2

Once again, if we searched our question with descriptors and roles, Document 2 would not have been retrieved because it is not on the subject. If both roles and links are used in a coordinate index, the role may be characterized as a letter prefix and the link as a number suffix, or vice versa. Another way of including roles in a coordinate index is to have a separate index unit for each descriptor and role combination as well as a separate descriptor without role for this term. Using the latter technique, five descriptors might appear in a coordinate index or the chemical Ethanol—"Ethanol (Reagent)," "Ethanol (Intermediate)," "Ethanol (Product)," "Ethanol (Solvent)," and "Ethanol (Role unspecified)." Should roles be used in an index to a personal document collection? Again, if searches are likely to yield few or no false drops without roles, then roles should not be included since they add to the over-all cost of the index.

Now to review the different types of logical searches that can be done with coordinate indexes. The two searches that illustrated false drops without links and roles, respectively, are examples of logical product searches. They were searches that specified the presence of all of the descriptors in documents that are to be retrieved. In the first search, relevant documents had to be indexed by descriptors "Republicans" *and* "Democratic candidates" *and* "U.S. presidency" *and* "Votes" *and* "1964."

The second search was for documents that were indexed with descriptors "Opinion polls" *and* "White" *and* "Negroes" *and* "Employment opportunities." An example of a logical sum search would be for documents indexed with descriptors "Employment opportunites" *or* "Foreign policy" *or* "Gun control." Notice that a search for the single, more generic descriptor "Issues" would achieve the same results. A logical difference search would be a search for documents that are indexed with the descriptor "Republicans" *but not* the descriptor "Democrats." A combination logical product, sum, and difference search would be a search for documents that are indexed with the descriptors "Opinion polls" *and* "Males" *and either* "Foreign policy" *or* "Taxes" *but not* "Gun control." Past studies of searches of coordinate indexes have shown that logical product searches and combination of logical products and logical sum searches are most common.

There are several variables that are independent of the forms of coordinate indexes. One of these variables is the provision of access points for other than the subject of the document. We have already mentioned two such types of access points. A date may be made an access point and this can be expressed as specifically as a particular day or even the time of a particular day or as generically as the century, depending on the needs of the index user. The date of either an event such as an opinion poll or the date of publication of a document or both dates can be indexed. The second type of access point other than the subject that has already been mentioned is the type or form of publication. This can be a review, an opinion poll, a legal document, a book or a part of a book, lecture notes, or any other type or form of document. Other access points that may be used are names of authors, a descriptor to indicate that the abstract of the document rather than the entire document is in the collection, and a descriptor to characterize a particularly important document. We will call each type of access point a descriptor. Descriptors for all but subjects and authors are likely to be auxiliary access points that will not be searched by themselves. Chances are that a search will not be made for all important documents or for all documents published on a certain date but for documents on a subject or an author that are considered important or are published on a certain date.

UNITERM INDEX

In a Uniterm index, document serial numbers representing documents that are indexed by a given descriptor are listed on a physical

Negroes

0	1	2	3	4	5	6	7	8	9
20	11	2	93		5	36	47	18	49
50	101	22	113		45	96	77	98	89
					85		127		

Opinion polls

0	1	2	3	4	5	6	7	8	9
10	21	2	3	4	5	36	27	78	49
30	41	22	43	24		86	57	118	69
50	71	52	83	34			87	128	99
90		102		64					
120									

Figure 5-2. Uniterm cards.

unit for that descriptor. The physical unit may be a card or a sheet of paper in either loose-leaf form or in a book. When the physical form is a card, it is called a Uniterm card. Uniterm cards for two descriptors from our political science index are given as Figure 5-2. One Uniterm card is prepared for each descriptor in the index. When that card is filled up with document serial numbers, a second card for that descriptor is prepared. The two illustrated cards represent more than the six document numbers that are in our sample collection. This is to illustrate both the posting (adding numbers onto the card) order and search procedure. The numbers on the Uniterm card are arranged by terminal digit (numbers ending with 0 are in the 0 column, numbers ending with 1 are in the 1 column, etc.) and in ascending number. To search a Uniterm index, two Uniterm cards are compared for common numbers. In our example, the common serial numbers for descriptors "Negroes" and "Opinion polls" are 2, 5, 36, 49, and 50 (the circled numbers). These matched serial numbers on two Uniterm cards represent the potentially pertinent documents for the two descriptors' logical product search. If the search is a logical product search of three descriptors, the matched serial numbers from the first two Uniterm cards are matched against the serial numbers on the third Uniterm card. This matching procedure is repeated with as many additional Uniterm cards as there are descriptors to coordinate.

The posting of document serial numbers on Uniterm cards can be done by handwriting, by typing, by using a numbering stamp or, for some of the larger collections, with the aid of data processing equipment. The Uniterm cards can be 3″ × 5″ in size as illustrated, 4″ × 6″, 5″ × 8″, or even larger cards. The individual Uniterm cards are usually filed alphabetically in a file box. Some of the larger indexes use mechanized rotary files or other filing aids that permit more rapid access to individual cards in the file but such devices are probably not necessary for personal indexes. The posting operation is a clerical one that is performed in the following way. We will assume that the document has been assigned a serial number as well as descriptors. The numbered and indexed document is taken to the file of Uniterm cards. Uniterm cards are pulled from the file for each of the descriptors used in the indexing of the document that is about to be posted. If a descriptor is used for the first time and no Uniterm card is in file for it, a new card is prepared by typing the descriptor on a blank card. The document serial number is posted by terminal digit on all Uniterm cards that have been pulled for this document. The descriptors listed on the document are then checked against the posted Uniterm cards to make sure that the posting has been completed. The Uniterm cards are then refiled alphabetically and the procedure is repeated for the next indexed document. The posting of document serial numbers is by terminal digit and in ascending numerical order to facilitate the number matching operation required when searching a Uniterm index. This arrangement of document serial numbers permits one to match numbers in one column of a Uniterm card against the numbers in a corresponding column of a second Uniterm card, a faster procedure than matching any number on one card against any number on a second card.

Each index unit in a Uniterm index, the Uniterm card, contains little information about any document—only the descriptor and the serial number of documents that are indexed by this descriptor. On the other hand, a loss of a Uniterm card may represent the loss of information that is time consuming to replace. One would have to look at every indexed document to determine whether or not it was posted on the lost Uniterm card. Uniterm cards can be made for authors, dates, types or forms of documents, documents not in collection, important documents, or any other access point that the user considers useful either by itself or in combination with another access point. Instead of making separate Uniterm cards for type or form of document, document not in file, or important document, other techniques can be used. A letter prefix or suffix can be used for this purpose or the document serial numbers can be written in different colors to indicate information about the indexed document. For example, a number in black might represent a journal article, while a red number might stand for part of a book, if this is a difference that is useful to bring out. Instead of using Uniterm cards to indicate the date of a document, the date may be derived from the serial number in some indexes. For example, document numbers 1 to 500 might represent documents published in 1967, document numbers 501 to 800 might be documents published in 1968, and so forth.

In searching, numbers on two Uniterm cards are best compared in one step. This represents either a logical product search for descriptor A *and* descriptor B, in which case serial numbers common to both cards are selected, or a logical difference search for descriptor A *but not* descriptor B in which case serial numbers that are on Uniterm card for descriptor A but not on Uniterm card for descriptor B are selected. A three-descriptor logical product or combination logical product and logical difference search is best done as a two-step operation, a four-descriptor logical product or combination logical product and logical difference search as a three-step operation, and so on. Logical sum searches do not require any matching of serial numbers. For example, a search for either descriptor A or descriptor B results in all of the serial numbers posted on Uniterm card for descriptor A and all serial numbers posted on Uniterm card for descriptor B. This type of search is not likely to occur frequently. A more common search is the combination logical product and logical sum search and it has to be converted into a logical product search. A search for descriptor A *and either* descriptor B *or* descriptor C *or* descriptor D must be converted into the three logical product searches for descriptor A *and* descriptor B, descriptor A *and* descriptor C, descriptor A *and* descriptor D.

Roles and links can be added to a Uniterm index as letter or number prefixes or suffixes to the posted document serial numbers as illustrated in our two sample searches. Roles can also be included by making separate Uniterm cards for descriptors with and without role combination. Descriptors for indexed documents can be eliminated by crossing out the document serial number on the appropriate Uniterm cards. New descriptors for indexed documents are added by posting the document serial number on the appropriate Uniterm cards. When this is done, care should be taken not to disturb the ordered arrangement of the document serial numbers on the Uniterm cards. This might mean re-arranging a column of numbers if the added document serial number represents a lower number than the last number posted in that column. Indexed documents can be removed from the index in one of several ways. The serial numbers of documents that are to be inactivated can be crossed out on the appropriate Uniterm cards; a list of cancelled document serial numbers can be kept and this list checked before retrieving potentially relevant documents identified in a search from the file; a "document cancelled" sheet can also be inserted in the file in the place of the inactivated document.

Uniterm indexes have been used with collections of 25,000 or more documents. The maximum useful document size depends upon the depth of the index, the number of descriptors in the index, the density of posting (number of serials numbers) of the most frequently used Uniterm cards, and the frequency of searching as well as the kinds of searches that are conducted. Chances are that the size of personal document collection under discussion is well within the optimum size of a Uniterm system.

Case Histories

A Uniterm index to a personal document collection of about 2500 documents in the field of chemical engineering is described by Cushing. The documents are indexed by over 7000 keywords (descriptors). The author does not use the published subject authority list in the field of chemical engineering since he does not believe that such a list is required for a one-man system. The index includes abstracts of documents, loose reprints, and articles in bound journals. Several suggestions are made by Cushing. Recurring (revised) documents as, for example, price lists, are given a single serial number which stands for the latest such document, the only one that is kept in the file. Some documents are best kept together by subject in a folder and when this is done, a serial number is assigned to the folder rather than to individual documents contained therein. Particularly important documents are indexed by the descriptor "fundamental." Roles are used in this system. It takes the author an average of 15 minutes per document to scan for keywords, posting and filing the document. It will take less time when articles to be included in the collection are already indexed by the authors, a procedure now used by some engineering journals. The types and frequency of searches conducted in this index are not mentioned.[3]

Wilkinson discusses Uniterm indexes maintained by chemists in an industrial laboratory. The index is on paper forms ($5'' \times 8''$) rather than on card stock with the forms filed in loose-leaf binders. Both author and subject indexes are used with the two indexes filed separately. A symbol is added to the document serial number to indicate documents in file. Drawings, graphs, and spectral charts can also be included in the index but do not have to be interfiled with other types of documents. No indexing or search times are given for the indexes.[4]

Cave describes the use of a Uniterm index for his collection of books on architecture. The index is on cards that are filed alphabetically. The author expresses satisfaction with his index but does not give details on size of collection, frequency of search, and other variables. No roles or links are used and false drops are not a problem in this index.[5]

Time for Mechanical Aspects of Indexing and Searching

Only the clerical or mechanical aspects of indexing and searching are discussed in this chapter since these aspects are performed differently with the three forms of coordinate indexes under discussion. The most extensive study of posting operations is reported by Gull. He assumes that 12,500 documents are already indexed (but not posted), requiring 100,000 Uniterm assignments and a vocabulary of 5000 descriptors. He is therefore discussing an index with an average depth of 8 descriptors per document. Time figures for the posting operation include the preparation of the Uniterm card the first time a descriptor is used; the location of the Uniterm card in the alphabetically arranged deck of cards (if a card has already been made for a descriptor); the posting of the serial number by terminal digit and in ascending numerical order; checking the Uniterm cards against descriptors noted on documents to insure completeness of posting; and refiling of Uniterm cards. For a collection of Uniterm cards filed alphabetically in boxes, an estimated 1.9 postings per minute can be made. The filing of the Uniterm cards on a mechanized rotary file or a visible card file results in a somewhat faster posting operation since less time is required for the location of the cards and because the cards are not removed from the file in the posting operation.[6] As was pointed out before, the activity of a personal index probably does not justify the investment in equipment for faster posting. The posting operation can thus be done at the rate of about 2 document serial numbers (on 2 Uniterm cards) per minute. There are no corresponding studies of the document serial number matching operation reported in the literature. In my experience, two heavily posted 5″ × 8″ Uniterm cards can be matched for common serial numbers in 2 minutes or less.

Equipment and Supplies

Uniterm cards can be prepared in the office from a ditto, mimeograph, or offset master marked with the ten-column arrangement of the Uniterm card. The master is then run off on index cards or slips of the proper size. Uniterm cards can also be purchased from the supplier listed below. If a numbering machine is to be used for posting document serial numbers, a model that can stamp the same number an unlimited number of times should be obtained. (A model that skips to the next number automatically is less than useful for posting.) If letter prefixes or suffixes are needed, one or more number wheels can be replaced with letter wheels in some stamping machines.

Suppliers of Equipment and Materials

Numbering machines.
Bates Manufacturing Company, 18 Central Avenue, West Orange, New Jersey 07051.
Remington Rand, Inc., Library Bureau Division, Herkimer, New York 13350.
Uniterm cards.
Documentation Inc., 4833 Rugby Avenue, Bethesda, Maryland 20014

OPTICAL COINCIDENCE SYSTEMS

The physical unit of the optical coincidence system is the optical coincidence card, also called, among other things, a Peek-a-boo card, a Batten card, or a Termatrex card (a trade name). As in the case of the Uniterm card, one optical coincidence card is made for each descriptor in the index. Unlike the Uniterm card, the document serial number of a document that is indexed by the descriptor is not posted on the card but is punched in it. Each optical coincidence card is divided into a number of positions and each position stands for a document serial number. This position is punched on an optical coincidence card when a document is indexed by this descriptor and it is left unpunched

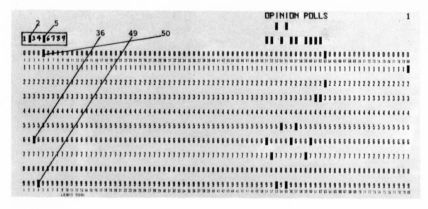

Figure 5-3.   Optical coincidence card.

when that document is not indexed by this descriptor. Figure 5-3 illustrates an optical coincidence card with 500 positions for the descriptor "Opinion polls" from our political science documents collection. The dedicated positions 2, 5, 36, 49, 50 are punched indicating that the corresponding documents deal with opinion polls. Optical coincidence cards come in different sizes and with different numbers of dedicated positions to accommodate 480 to 40,000 document serial numbers. The individual cards are usually filed alphabetically, although some of the larger systems use a random arrangement of cards with cards being selected from the file by means of a colored tab or other selection device. In searching, two or more optical coincidence cards that are to be matched for common serial numbers are superimposed and the holes that can be seen through the superimposed cards represent document serial numbers that share the matched or coordinated descriptors. The holes are then translated into document serial numbers and the selected documents are retrieved from the file. The mechanics of searching an optical coincidence system are illustrated in Figure 5-4.

The individual optical coincidence card contains little information (as does the Uniterm card): only the descriptor and document serial numbers that are indexed by it. Again, the loss of an optical coincidence card can be time consuming to replace since each document needs to be checked to determine whether or not it was indexed and punched on the lost optical coincidence card. As in the case of the Uniterm system, optical coincidence cards can be prepared for any type of descriptor that might appear desirable. Information about documents can also be indexed by means of a color code. Let us say that we want to specify important documents on a subject. To do this we will use an optical coincidence card of the same size as the cards in the rest of the deck but this card will be made of a red translucent plastic. We will punch this card in the dedicated position for any document that is considered particularly important. When searching, this card will be superimposed along with the subject cards. White holes that are seen through the superimposed cards represent serial numbers of important and potentially relevant documents (those for which the red plastic card has been punched) while red holes represent the serial numbers of other, potentially relevant documents. This device helps to determine how many important documents there are on a subject. If there are few important documents we might look at the other documents as well. If there are many important documents for this search, we may only want to look at those. Colored codes can also be used for types of publications, and for deleted documents, as we shall see below. Descriptor links cannot be provided with an optical coincidence system but documents can be broken down into smaller units if false drop problems are anticipated. Roles are provided by means of two or more optical coincidence cards for descriptors with role combinations and for descriptors without a role. With the Uniterm system only two descriptors could be coordinated at one time for either a logical product or a logical difference search. This is not a limitation with an optical coincidence system. As many descriptors as are required in a search can be

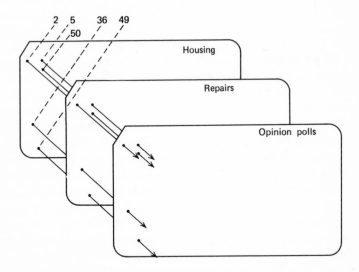

Figure 5-4.   Searching an optical coincidence system.

coordinated in a single-step logical product search. It is simply a matter of superimposing as many optical coincidence cards as there are descriptors to be coordinated. A two-descriptor logical difference can also be done in one step. If we make a search for descriptor A but not descriptor B, we superimpose the optical coincidence card for descriptor A on the optical coincidence card for descriptor B. Holes in the descriptor A card that are blocked by cardstock of the descriptor B card represent the document numbers that are indexed with descriptor A but not descriptor B. The same searching technique can be used for a combination logical product and single-descriptor logical difference search. If we want to search descriptors A and B and C and D but not E, we place the optical coincidence card for descriptor E on the bottom of the deck and superimpose the optical coincidence cards for descriptors A, B, C, and D in no particular order. The holes that can be seen through optical coincidence descriptors cards A, B, C, and D but are blocked by optical coincidence card for descriptor E represent serial numbers of potentially relevant documents for this search. Logical sum searches are conducted by identifying serial numbers on two or more individual optical coincidence cards. Combination of logical product and sum searches have to be converted into logical product searches, as in the case of the Uniterm system. Addition of descriptors to indexed documents is easily accomplished. The appropriate optical coincidence cards are punched for the particular document number. Deletion of descriptors from indexed documents is done by "stuffing" the hole for the document number on the optical coincidence card. Mistakes in punching cards are also corrected in this way. The same technique can also be used to remove a document from the index. Another way to do this is to have a colored optical coincidence card, as previously mentioned, and to punch this card for the document number that is to be removed. The "document removed" card is always used in searching. If it is a green card and a green hole can be seen through the superimposed deck of optical coincidence cards, this would be an indication that the document is still in the collection. If a white hole shines through, this means that the "document removed" card has been punched for that document number and that the document is no longer in file. Still another way to indicate that a document has been inactivated is to place a "document removed" card in its place in the file.

One set of optical coincidence cards can be used for as many documents as there are dedicated positions on each card. When there are 480 such positions, then a second set of optical coincidence cards has to be prepared when the collection grows to 481 documents, and a third set when the collection reaches 961 documents, and so on. A set of optical coincidence cards with 40,000 dedicated positions is good until the document collection reaches 40,001 documents. The anticipated maximum size of the collection will be one of the determining factors in selecting a particular type of optical coincidence card. It should be pointed out that the cost of the card and the equipment needed for punching holes on the card usually increases as the capacity of the card increases.

Case Histories

One of the earliest applications of the optical coincidence index is described by Batten. He used the system to index a collection of patents in the field of plastics. A homemade $8'' \times 10''$ card with 400 positions was used at first and then replaced by Hollerith (IBM) cards with 800 positions (10 punches for each of the 80 columns). Documents are indexed by chemical names, processes, and uses of plastics. Each of the three types of subject descriptors are characterized by a number from a classification system. The number serves as the heading for each optical coincidence card. Names of individual inventors or inventing companies are also indexed. Optical coincidence cards are made for the more frequently used author and company names. Other author and company names are indexed on optical coincidence cards made for each letter of the alphabet. This has resulted in some false drops but these proved to be easy to separate. At the time of the writing (1951), 6800 documents were included in the system on 14 sets of optical coincidence cards, 10 sets of 400 position cards and 4 sets of 800 position cards. The author states that an index to 800 patents on one card can, in most cases, be sorted in 10 minutes.[7] This, I believe, is a case of typical British understatement and assumes that the searcher has a cup of tea in the process.

Starker and Cordero describe the use of an optical coincidence card system used for scientists' personal document or data collections. The standard 80-column IBM tabulating card is used as the optical coincidence card. The document serial number is punched as a single hole in rows 0 to 9 on columns 1 to 50 except for document numbers 1 through 9. The first or first and second digit of the document number is indicated by the column number and the last digit is indicated by the row number. Document number 96, for example, is punched as the 6 punch in column 9; document number 468 is punched as the 8 punch in column 46. Document numbers 1 through 9 are punched as "11" punches in columns 1 through 9. One set of optical coincidence cards can hold up to 500 document serial numbers. The serial numbers are keypunched as are the descriptors that are punched in columns 51 to 79. Column 80 is reserved to indicate the set number. A "1" punch in column 80 indicates the first set of cards, those containing document numbers 1 through 500; a "2" punch in column 80 indicates the second set of cards, those containing document numbers 501 through 1000, etc. The different decks of cards are also differentiated by the use of different color tabulating cards. The cards can be reproduced mechanically when they wear out or when multiple sets of cards are needed, which happens when the personal index of one researcher is shared by another researcher. The largest document collection indexed with this system consists of 4000 documents punched on 8 sets of descriptor cards. For searching this collection, 8 separate subsearches have to be made, something that might become unwieldy if many searches need to be conducted. Starker and Cordero suggest as a rule of thumb that when the number of daily searches multiplied by the number of sets of card decks that have to be searched exceeds 10, thought should be given to a new and more effective search tool. An IBM Port-a-Punch deck with 480 prescored holes per card was considered before deciding on the standard IBM card. The decision not to use the Port-a-Punch cards was made because the manual punching operation was awkward and because the Port-a-Punch cards could not be readily reproduced mechanically.[8]

Mount relates an industrial library's experience with an optical coincidence system to a collection of reports. A 9″ × 11″ Termatrex card with space for 10,000 documents per card was used. Indexable information for any document was recorded on a worksheet. To save time, the worksheet listed the 50 most commonly used descriptors. These descriptors were checked off on the worksheet at a saving in time over writing. A colored plastic card is used to characterize cancelled documents. The cost of the Termatrex punching and searching equipment came to about $1400. Cards cost $.25 each and a card holder for 1500 cards is $45.[9]

Time for Mechanical Aspects of Indexing and Searching

Studies of card-punching speeds for optical coincidence systems that did not use standard keypunches for tabulating cards are reported by Gull,[10] Linder,[11] and Mount.[12] The figures ranged from $3\frac{1}{2}$ to 5 minutes for punching an average of 8 optical coincidence cards per document. The time includes the pulling of the optical coincidence cards from the file, punching the set of cards for the document number, verifying the punch, and refiling the cards. Search time for the document collection on the 10,000 document number Termatrex cards used by Mount is reported in another article. For a single logical product search with one set of cards, it takes about 15 seconds to select each card, 15 seconds to identify each hole (to translate it into a corresponding document serial number), and 15 seconds to refile each card. For example, a four-descriptor logical product search in which 10 potentially relevant documents are identified would take $3\frac{1}{2}$ minutes.[13]

Suppliers of Materials and Equipment

Find-It, P. O. Box 25942, West Los Angeles Station, Los Angeles, California 90025.
Jonker Business Machines, 26 N. Summit Avenue, Gaithersburg, Maryland 20760.
McBee Systems, Division of Litton Industries, Port Chester, New York   10573.

EDGE-NOTCHED CARDS

Edge-notched cards, also called hand-sorted punched cards, are index cards of various sizes with one or more rows of holes around the periphery. It is the holes in the card that makes the difference. The holes are given meanings or, to put it differently, each descriptor in the index is characterized as a single hole or a combination of holes on the card. One card is prepared for each document included in the index. The cards are punched by removing the piece of cardboard between the hole and the edge of the card. There are two possibilities per hole: either the hole is punched or it is not punched. The hole is punched on a card if it represents a descriptor used in indexing the document for which it stands. It is not punched when the descriptor does not apply for a given document. Figure 5-5 represents the punched edge-notched card for Document 5 in our political science collection.

The searching of a deck of edge-notched cards consists of separating cards that are punched for certain holes from cards that are not so punched. The cards that are punched in designated holes represent potentially relevant documents for logical product or logical sum searches. For logical difference searches, cards are selected that are not punched in designated positions. The mechanics of sorting will be illustrated for a search of documents on opinion polls which, in our collection, are documents punched in hole 87. We take about 200 cards at a time (or fewer cards if we do not have that many documents in the collection) and insert a sorting needle, which looks like an icepick, through hole 87 in all of the cards. The needle with the cards is raised about a foot over the sorting surface (a table or desk will do nicely). When

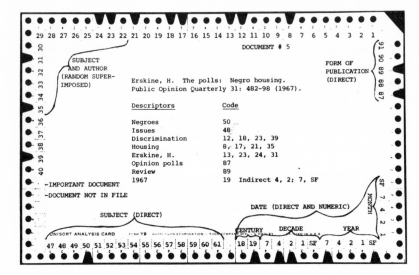

Figure 5-5. Edge-notched punched card.

the cards are lifted with the needle, cards that are punched in hole 87 will have no physical support and will, therefore, fall from the needle. They will fall from the needle unless they are held up by adjoining cards that do not have the sorted hole punched. To prevent such cards from staying on the needle, the deck of cards is fanned out evenly over the entire length of the needle. The cards that fall from the sorting needle represent the potentially relevant documents. If there are more than about 200 cards in the index, the search has to be continued for each additional set of about 200 cards. Also, cards selected during the first sort might have to be sorted again for holes that stand for additional descriptors. When more than one descriptor needs to be coordinated and the descriptors to be coordinated are represented by holes on the same edge of the card, two or more needles can be used in a single sort. More about this later.

Coding

The assignment of meanings to individual holes or groups of holes on the edge-notched cards is called coding. We can assign any meaning to any hole or combination of holes. The trick is to make good use of the available coding space on the cards, which on our illustrated 5″ × 8″ card consists of 97 holes. By good use we mean the selection of a code that is as simple to punch and sort as possible, that allows space for all of the descriptors now included in the index and all the descriptors that are likely to be needed during the useful life of the index. And this is not easy. We will discuss several types of codes and then go through the steps of developing a code for our index to political science documents.

Direct Code

The simplest code to punch and to sort is one in which one meaning is assigned to each hole, the direct code. This was already illustrated when we used hole 87 to represent the descriptor "Opinion polls." Unfortunately, the direct code usually does not satisfy the requirement of providing enough space for all the descriptors that are now in the system or are likely to be needed in the system. If we could anticipate a maximum of 97 or fewer descriptors for our political science index, we would code each descriptor by means of a direct code. It should be pointed out that space for a descriptor must be provided on every card whether or not the descriptor is used on that card, hence the limitation of 97 descriptors with a direct code for a card of this size. Usually many more descriptors are needed and for this reason the direct code is used in conjunction with indirect codes.

Indirect Codes

To get around the limitation of insufficient coding possibilities with a direct code, two or more holes can be given a single meaning. Two of the more common types of indirect codes, as these types of codes are called, will be discussed. They are the numeric and the random superimposed code.

Before we continue with the discussion of codes, one additional term needs to be defined. A group of holes used for a particular purpose on an edge-notched card is called a code field. In the first numeric code that we will discuss we will use a four-hole code field for designating any one single digit from 1 to 9. The four holes in the code field will be labelled 7, 4, 2, 1, respectively, and will also have the corresponding numeric value. By punching either one or two holes in this code field, any one number from 1 to 9 will be characterized. For 1, hole 1 is punched; for 2, hole 2 is punched; for 3, holes 2 and 1 are punched; for 4, hole 4 is punched; for 5, holes 4 and 1 are punched; for 6, holes 4 and 2 are punched; for 7, hole 7 is punched; for 8, holes 7 and 1 are punched; and for 9, holes 7 and 2 are punched. We can also designate the digit 0 by an absence of punches in the four-hole code field.

With this code, we can punch and, therefore, sort 9 digits with a four-hole code field instead of a nine-hole code field that would be required with a direct code. The saving of five holes over the direct code is not all profit. We pay for it by spending additional time in punching and sorting the cards. Also, we can only punch a single number in any 7, 4, 2, 1 code field. If we assign more than one number, we will get what are called "mechanical false drops" or, simply, false drops, if you do not care how you obtain nonrelevant documents. An example will illustrate. Let us assume that we want to punch two numbers, number 5 and number 9, in a single 7, 4, 2, 1 code field. For number 5, we will punch holes 4 and 1; for number 9, we punch holes 7 and 2. If we sort the deck that contains this card for number 5 or for number 9, we will get this card and that is as it should be. However, we will also get this card if we sort in this code field for numbers 1 or 2 or 3 or 4 or 6 or 7 or 8 even though chances are that we will not be interested in this card when we are sorting for numbers other than 5 or 9. The reason for the false drops is that when punching for the second number we have unintentionally punched the card for all other code combinations. This would not happen with a direct code since each hole is coded independently of any other hole on the card and as many directly coded holes can be punched on any card as are necessary for indexing that document.

There is another sorting problem with the 7, 4, 2, 1 code, but it is one that can be corrected by assigning a fifth hole to the code field. If we sort for the number 7 by inserting the needle in hole 7, we will not only get cards that are coded with the number 7 in the code field but also cards that have the hole 7 punched as part of a number, namely the number 8 (7 and 1) and number 9 (7 and 2). The same holds true for numbers 4, 2, and 1. The unwanted cards can be separated mechanically, in the case of the number 7 code, by sorting the deck of cards in the 1 position and keeping the cards that remain on the needle and then sorting the deck in the 2 position, again keeping the cards that remain on the needle. The need for multiple sorting of a single digit in a numeric code can be eliminated for all but the digit 0 by adding a fifth hole to the code field and punching this hole (called SF, or single figure) whenever the number 7 or 4 or 2 or 1 is coded. In this way, each digit except 0 is characterized by a unique two-hole combination that can be sorted with two needles in one pass. The digit 0 is represented by the absence of punches in the code field. The digit 0 is sorted by first sorting hole "1" of the 7, 4, 2, 1 code field and keeping the cards that remain on the needle (the cards that are not punched in that hole). These cards are then sorted sequentially on the other three holes, keeping in each sort the cards that remain on the needle. The 7, 4, 2, 1 code with or without an SF hole can be modified by adding a sixth hole to characterize the number 0. This eliminates the need for sorting for the absence of a punch in the code field. Another modification, not particularly recommended, is the coding of any number from 1 to 14 in the code field by using up to four holes (the maximum is used for the number 14) for any code. It is not recommended because it adds both to the punching and sorting time. A better way of increasing the code capacity is the use of two or more 7, 4, 2, 1 (again with or without SF) code fields in combination. Two such code fields combined into a single code field of 8 or 10 holes can be used to code any number from 1 to 99, three such code fields used in combination can be used to code any one number from 1 to 999, etc. An eight- or ten-hole code field is used at times for coding the date of a document with the decade being coded in one 7, 4, 2, 1 type code field and the year in another such code field. Again, only one number can be coded in any one code field because of the false drop problem already mentioned.

Random Superimposed Code

There is another type of indirect code that can be used when the restriction of a single descriptor (number) assignment to any one document in any one indirect numeric code field is unacceptable. This is the random superimposed code. It is called superimposed because the codes for two or more descriptors for a document can be punched into a single code field by superimposing one coding pattern upon another. (The use of two or more punches in a code field is called a code pattern.) It is called random because the numbers for the coding positions are selected at random, for reasons that will be explained below. When two or more coding patterns are coded in a single random superimposed code field, there is a possibility of a mechanical false drop when the deck is searched for code patterns that are made up from parts of code patterns that are punched in the card. False drops can be kept to an acceptable maximum by judicious code design. Part of the trick is to select numbers at random for the code pattern so that no one number is selected more frequently than another number. (While this makes for random *selection* of numbers for code patterns, it does not prevent the numbers from being punched more frequently than other numbers because some descriptors are *used* more frequently than others. This is not likely to be a problem in an index to a small documents collection.) An example of the use of a random superimposed code field of 40 positions with a coding pattern of four holes per descriptor is illustrated in Figure 5-5. In this code field the descriptors "Discrimination," "Housing," and the name of the author, H. Erskine, are entered. While the illustrated code utilizes a forty-position code field and a code pattern of four punches per descriptor, other code field and code pattern sizes can be used. The code design should take into consideration the number of possible coding patterns in a code field, the minimum and maximum number of descriptors coded in any one code field, and the maximum acceptable number of false drops when searching the code field with one or more descriptors. Bourne provides a formula for using these variables to determine both the desirable size of the code field and the number of punches per code pattern. He also calculates that the forty-hole code field with four-hole code pattern gives 91,390 unique code possibilities, which should be enough for most personal indexes. In the same report he states that the code is used most efficiently when half of the holes are punched on any one card. This would provide an average of 6 descriptors rather than 5 for the 20 punches since the descriptors are likely to share some punches.[14] There is, of course, no harm in using fewer descriptors per code field. With an index of the size under discussion, an average of 6 descriptors punched in a random superimposed code is not likely to yield a large number of false drops, particularly if two or more descriptors are searched in this field for any one search. An example of the use of a forty-hole code field with four-hole code pattern random superimposed code on an edge-notched card somewhat different than the one illustrated is given by Mooers.[15]

Author Codes

Authors' names can be coded in a random superimposed code field. They can also be translated as numbers and coded into a 7, 4, 2, 1 type of code field or coded as letters. Two types of author codes are illustrated in Figures 5-6 and 5-7. The letter P is punched in both of these code fields. Three such code fields would be required for coding three letters of an author's name. In a small file, a single letter or two letters may be sufficient for the author code. This will not permit a sort for the specific author but it is likely to eliminate most of the unwanted cards. The final sort is a manual operation that should not take long. Using 15 or 24 positions, respectively, for a three-letter author code may be more space than one wants to devote to an author code, hence we suggest coding a single letter or including the author's name in the random superimposed code field when one is available for use. In the latter case, more than one author's name can be entered in the

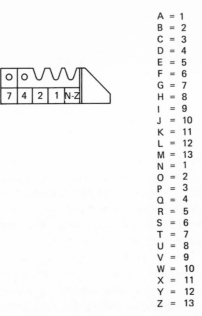

A = 1
B = 2
C = 3
D = 4
E = 5
F = 6
G = 7
H = 8
I = 9
J = 10
K = 11
L = 12
M = 13
N = 1
O = 2
P = 3
Q = 4
R = 5
S = 6
T = 7
U = 8
V = 9
W = 10
X = 11
Y = 12
Z = 13

Figure 5-6. Author code with 7, 4, 2, 1, N-Z code field.

code field. Again it is not all profit since the author's name has to be translated into the coding positions which is an extra step that is not needed in the two illustrated author codes.

Cards with Multiple Rows of Holes

A second row of holes doubles the number of coding positions on a card. A third row of holes triples the coding position as compared with a single-rowed card. In the case of a double-rowed card, the outer row is used in the same way as in the single-rowed card. The inner row is coded by separating the cardboard between the two inner and

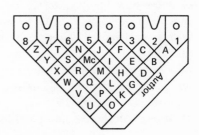

Figure 5-7. Author code with 8 position letter code field.

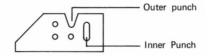

Figure 5-8.   Shallow and inner punch in double rowed edge-notched card.

outer holes as illustrated in Figure 5-8. Sorting for the inner hole is performed by first inserting the needle into the inner hole on a deck of about 200 cards. Cards that are punched in this position will not drop from the deck but will be lowered by a fraction of an inch in comparison with the other cards on the needle. The lowered cards are separated from the other cards on the needle by first inserting a second needle in one corner of the lowered cards (this keeps them together), and then by removing the original sort needle from the entire deck to separate the cards to be selected from the rest of the deck. A triple-rowed card has a second intermediate punching position per hole, the space between the innermost hole and the intermediate hole. Sorting for these positions is similar to sorting the inner row of holes in a double-rowed card. Other types of codes, and other sorting techniques including the sorting of cards with a 7, 4, 2, 1 code in numeric order, are discussed in detail in a book by Casey et al.[16]

Code Design

The steps for developing a code for an index on edge-notched cards will now be discussed with the aid of our political science document collection. A code should not be designed until indexable information has been selected for at least several hundred documents. This is because we need some evidence on which to base our decisions. Let us therefore assume that indexable information has been selected for about 500 documents. In code design, a decision has to be made on what types of access points are needed and an estimate made of the number of different units to expect for each type of access point. For example, we need to guess how many different descriptors will be required in the subject index since we will have to allot coding space for every existing as well as anticipated descriptor. Since this step is somewhat akin to crystal-ball gazing, the probability of poor guessing is compensated by providing what might be termed a contingency. A portion of the holes on the card is therefore saved for future and unpredicted expansion.

In our example, we have decided that we require access points by subject, author, type of publication, and date. Also, a code is desired to indicate important documents on a subject and documents for which only the abstract rather than the entire document is available. A couple of reminders: the most commonly indexed and searched descriptors should also be the easiest to punch and to sort. A code field of the 7, 4, 2, 1 type can only be coded with one number on any one code field.

There are now several hundred subject descriptors in the index. This number is expected to increase to several thousand subject descriptors. Ten of the existing descriptors are expected to be used most commonly in indexing and sorting. These are therefore assigned 10 holes for the direct coding. Fifteen holes are reserved for direct coding of the most important subject descriptors, to allow for expansion in the number of such descriptors. The other subject descriptors are expected to be used at the rate of about 4 or 5 per document. We cannot break down these descriptors into mutually exclusive groups and, therefore, a code other than a 7, 4, 2, 1 type code must be used. Since we do not have enough holes for direct coding of these subject descriptors, we will use a random superimposed code. A 40-position code field with a code pattern made up of 4 positions per descriptor is selected since it gives a large enough number of coding possibilities and a probability of a low percentage of false drops with the anticipated use of the code field. There are five types of publications that we would like to code. Types of publications will be characterized for each document and are expected to be used frequently in searching. A 5-hole direct code field is therefore assigned for this purpose. We do not expect any need for expansion for the "type of publication" code field and are therefore not leaving any additional holes for this purpose. If our guess turns out to be incorrect, unassigned expansion positions may be used to expand this code field. We are also assigning direct codes for both the "important document" descriptor and the "document not in collection" descriptor but for a different reason. These descriptors are not likely to be used frequently in indexing, particularly not the "important document" descriptor since it would otherwise lose its discriminating value, but these descriptors will be used frequently in searching. Only one date will be punched per document and this information can therefore be coded in part with a 7, 4, 2, 1, SF code. The coding of the decade, year, and month with an indirect code can be done at a saving of 17 holes over the direct code and that is a saving worth considering. The century will be coded directly with 2 holes assigned the meaning 1800 and 1900, respectively. Some documents also require a code for the month of the year and this will be made possible by means of a modified 7, 4, 2, 1, SF code field. The modification is made to accommodate the extra two coding positions, 11 and 12, for November and December, respectively. The number 11 is characterized by a punch in the 7 and 4 positions. This combination of holes has not been used for any other codes. The number 12 will be characterized by punches in the 7, 4, and 1 holes. The code for number 12 includes the codes for number 5 (4 and 1) and number 8 (7 and 1) as well as number 11 (7 and 4). We will, therefore, have to eliminate cards punched for 12 when sorting for number 5, 8, and 11 and do so either manually or mechanically. We do not expect to include in the index any documents published before 1800. Also, we do not expect our index to survive beyond the year 2000. Instead of coding the authors' names in a separate code field which would require at least 5 holes for a single letter code field, we have decided to code the author's name in the random superimposed code field. This is one of the advantages of a superimposed code field. One can insert almost anything.

To sum up, we have made the following use of the holes on our card.

Subject	Direct code	15 holes
Subject and author	Random superimposed code	40 holes
Type of publication	Direct code	5 holes
Important document	Direct code	1 hole
Document not in file	Direct code	1 hole
Date	Direct code and 7, 4, 2, 1, SF code	17 holes
	Total number of holes used	79

Thus, 79 out of 97 holes have been assigned, giving us 18 holes for as yet unforeseen needs.

On the one card that is made up for each document, either an abstract of the document can be added or a microfilm of the entire document can be inserted. The edge-notched card system thus provides more information per index unit than either the Uniterm or the optical coincidence card. A loss of a single card means the loss of the index for a document, which may or may not be serious. The same types of descriptors can be provided for this form of coordinate index as for the other two forms that have been discussed, as long as the required coding space has been provided. We cannot specify how many descriptors can be coordinated in one step since this depends on the code that is used. If a direct code is used and if 6 descriptors that are characterized by single punches on one edge of the card need to be searched in a 6-descriptor logical product search, then all 6 descriptors can be coordinated in a single step (though only about 200 cards can be sorted in each step). If, on the other hand, a descriptor has to be sorted that is characterized by means of an indirect code, then the sort for a single descriptor may have to be a multiple-step operation. Each logical sum search requires one or more separate sorting steps. Logical difference searches are conducted by sorting the hole or holes for descriptors that should not be indexed in a document. The cards that remain on the needle (the unpunched cards for that particular hole or holes) are the potentially relevant documents rather than the cards that drop from the deck as was the case for the logical product and logical sum searches. Links cannot be added to an edge-notched card system. Roles are added in the same way as for the optical coincidence system—by having separate codes for each descriptor role and descriptor without role combination. Adding descriptors to indexed documents is a matter of adding the appropriate punch or punches to the card for the document. Deleting a descriptor from an indexed document is done by making a new edge (covering the hole) by means of adhesive paper prepared for this purpose and called a card saver. Errors in punching a card are corrected in the same way. The removal of a document from the collection is done by withdrawing the card for the document that is to be deleted. The edge-notched card system is the only one of the three forms of coordinate indexes with a maximum size limitation that may be lower than the anticipated maximum size of the personal indexes under discussion. Experience has shown that edge-notched card systems come close to their maximum useful size when they approach 5000 documents. The maximum size may even be reached sooner. The mechanics of sorting a large deck of cards are cumbersome and discouraging when the collection approaches 5000 documents and the same number of cards since only about 200 cards can be sorted at one time.

Case Histories

Milne and Milne report on 12 years of experience with an index on edge-notched cards to the literature on vision and its uses in invertebrate animals. At the time the article was written, 4500 cards were in the index. A $7\frac{1}{2}'' \times 3\frac{1}{4}''$ single-rowed card with 80 holes is used. Sixteen holes are used for direct coding of subjects. Thirty-four holes are used for a 7, 4, 2, 1 taxonomic code, based on the Dewey Decimal Classification system. Twenty holes are used for an indirect 7, 4, 2, 1 plus N-Z hole code for indexing the author's name by means of the first four letters of the senior author's last name. The date is punched with a 7, 4, 2, 1 code for the decade and year and a single direct punch to characterize documents published before 1900. A single direct hole is used to note that an abstract has been prepared for the document. If the code were to be revised after 12 years of experience, the following changes are suggested by the authors. A larger card with more coding space would be used. The taxonomic classification system was not useful for searching purposes and would, therefore, be omitted. More direct coding positions are needed for coding subjects and this code field would be increased from 16 to 31 holes. The date code would be modified by adding a direct hole for the twentieth century. The bibliographic code would be expanded by adding directly coded positions to indicate that a document is in file as a full-sized document or in microform. A three-letter indirect code for the journal title would also be added since this would facilitate a frequently conducted type of search that is now difficult to perform.[17]

Hinde describes an index to a collection of documents on gas kinetics and free radical reactions. A single-rowed card 4″ × 6″ in size, with 70 holes, was used. The size of the document collection is not indicated. Direct codes are used for the type of paper (e.g., theoretical, experimental), type of chemistry (e.g., analytical), type of publication, and for each of the following three meanings: reprint in file, of teaching interest, idea suggested by reading paper. The author's name is punched with a direct letter code for the first letter of the author's last name. A direct code field is also assigned for dates but, for the sake of economy of space, a range of years rather than a single year is coded in each of the five holes. The inclusive number of years covered in this code can be increased by converting the code from a direct one to a numeric one. Specific subjects are coded in three 7, 4, 2, 1 numeric code fields. Both specific and generic subjects are indexed, with the generic subjects searched primarily in combination with each other or with specific subjects.[18]

Hoff describes an index to health education information which makes use of a single-rowed 5″ × 8″ edge-notched punched card with 122 holes. The descriptors are preprinted on the card for ease of coding and the cards are available from Health Education Resources and Consultation, a supplier listed below. Direct codes are used for form of publication, subject discipline, human behavioral concepts, type of information included in document (e.g., costs, methods, history, economic status, and age groups). Health subjects are coded indirectly. Each of the 19 holes in the health subject code field is assigned two meanings and an additional hole is used to indicate which of the two meanings applies on any one card. For example, one hole is assigned the meanings "Food" and "Water." When "Water" is to be coded on a card, only a single hole is punched. When "Food" is coded, the same hole as for "Water" plus another hole are punched to signify that the alternate meaning applies. The author's name is coded with a two hole punch in an eight-hole code field that was illustrated in Figure 5-7. An indirect code field is also used for coding the date.[19]

Harris and Wallace describe an index for which 3″ × 5″ single-rowed edge-notched cards are used for two separate document collections, a 1400 document collection in the field of inorganic chemistry and a 2000 document collection in the field of analytical chemistry. The card is divided into five code fields. Field 1 contains the general subject or subjects of the document, coded directly; field 2 contains the experimental technique used, also coded directly; field 3 represents the periodic table which is coded by means of a combination direct and indirect code; field 4 has the author and date also coded with a combination direct and indirect code; in field 5, subjects coded generically in fields 1 to 3 are coded specifically in a random superimposed code field. A number of holes is kept unused for future expansion.[20]

Thoma describes an index in the field of biochemistry that makes use of a random superimposed code on a double-rowed 3″ × 5″ edge-notched card. The system is of interest because it utilizes a self-demarking word code. Each word (descriptor) is coded by a two letter-number set. The author claims that the coding technique can be committed to memory in a matter of minutes. He states that words are coded at the rate of 2 to 4 words per minute and that searching takes 2 to 3 minutes per deck of 1000 cards. False drops are not a problem with an average code density of 5 words per card.[21]

In summary, experience of users of edge-notched card systems for personal indexes seems to indicate that the code should be kept as simple as possible and the temptation resisted to make the system do what is not needed. The code should not be designed until a representative number of documents has been indexed and the deck of cards becomes cumbersome to handle when it approaches 5000 cards.

Time for Clerical and Mechanical Aspects of Indexing and Searching

The clerical aspects of index preparation consist of writing or typing the bibliographic citation and other information on the edge-notched card for the document, translating the descriptors into coding position on the card, punching the card, and verifying the punches for correctness and completeness. No time figures are available for writing or typing on the edge-notched cards but the copying of a bibliographic citation on any piece of paper takes about 1 to 2 minutes. No time figures are available for translating the descriptors into coding positions for punching the cards or for verifying the punches. In some cases, the descriptors are identified on the edge-notched cards and when this is so the translation is done without a code dictionary. The mechanical input time will also depend on the number of punches required per card. The average mechanical input time for an edge-punched card system is probably about the same as for a Uniterm or an optical coincidence system, about 5 minutes per document. The mechanical sorting time is slower for the edge-punched card system. In one report, cards were sorted at the rate of about 200 cards per minute for a single sort. The sort was for either a single hole or for several holes on one side of the card.[22] Higher sorting figures have been reported by a manufacturer of edge-notched cards. The Royal-McBee Company reports that 60,000 single-hole sorts per hour (1000 cards per minute for a single hole) are considered average, although 90,000 single-hole sorts per hour have frequently been reported.[23] These higher sorting rates are possible when done on a production basis by experienced sorters aided by mechanical sorting devices sold by the manufacturers of the edge-notched cards. For personal indexes, the lower sorting figure is probably more realistic. It should also be remembered that most searches will require multiple sorts of the deck. The second and subsequent sorts are, however, for only a fraction of the deck since the bulk of the cards will have been rejected in the first sort.

Equipment and Supplies

The basic supplies of the edge-notched card system are the cards, a card file, a punch, and one or more sorting needles. In its least expensive form, the card file, the punching and sorting equipment can be obtained at the local dime store for an investment under $5.00. A conductor's punch can serve for punching the holes, an icepick (with a dulled point as a safety measure) or a knitting needle can be used for sorting the deck of cards. A somewhat higher investment, of about $50.00, will purchase a chrome-plated punch with a receptacle for the edges of paper that are clipped away, sorting needles especially designed for this purpose, and a sorting block for easier alignment of the cards. Cards can be homemade from index cards, if you have the time, skill, and inclination,[24] or purchased from one of the suppliers listed below. These suppliers will usually have both cards as well as sorting and punching equipment. The price per card will vary depending on the size of the card, the number of holes per card, and the number of cards bought at a time. Estimate paying about $.05 per card.

Suppliers of Materials and Equipment

Burroughs Corp., 1150 University Avenue, Rochester, New York   14605.
E-Z Sort Systems, 45 2nd Street, San Francisco, California   91346.
Health Education Resources and Consultation, 6049 Skyline Boulevard, Oakland,
    California   94611 (descriptors for health education subjects printed on cards).
McBee Systems, Division of Litton Industries, Port Chester, New York   10573.

SUMMARY

Some of the characteristics of the three coordinate indexes that have just been discussed are summarized in Figure 5-9. Little or no equipment is required for any of the three indexes and each of them can be used at one's desk. These are two of the principal reasons why they have been discussed in this chapter. There are advantages and disadvantages for each of the three forms of coordinate indexes. While the index on edge-notched punched cards provides more information per index unit than either of the two other indexes, it requires the most time for the mechanical aspects of searching. The optical coincidence system is fastest to search and gives immediate feedback on the number of potentially relevant documents in a search. This makes possi-

	Form of index		
Characteristics	Uniterm	Optical coincidence	Edge-notched cards
Order of file	Document numbers on descriptor cards	Document numbers on descriptor cards	Descriptor on document cards
Amount of information per card	Document number only	Document number only	Up to entire document
Provision of roles	Yes	Yes	Yes
Provision of links	Yes	No	No
Number of descriptors that can be coordinated in a one-step logical product search	Two	As many as are required in one search	May be fewer than two, depending on code used

Figure 5-9. Comparison of some of the characteristics of Uniterm, optical coincidence and edge-notched card systems.

ble the readjustment of the search by coordinating one or more additional descriptor cards if too many holes show through the superimposed cards, by removing one or more descriptor cards if not enough holes show through. The optical coincidence card system does have the disadvantage of requiring a new set of cards whenever the document collection goes past the capacity of the card. This is not likely to be a problem if a card with a capacity of 10,000 positions is used (the more expensive system) but may be a problem with a card that has a 500-position limit. The Uniterm system requires no expenditure in equipment if index cards are converted into Uniterm cards and if the document numbers are either handwritten or typed. But searching the Uniterm card is a slower process than searching a deck of optical coincidence cards. It is possible to have a combination Uniterm and optical coincidence system but this is not recommended.

Should a coordinate index be used for a personal documents collection? If an index of some depth, say eight or more descriptors per document, including authors and other access points, is required, the answer is, probably, yes. Conventional indexes of comparable depth are more expensive to prepare because they require a larger number of physical index units. Also, conventional indexes do not offer as much searching flexibility as coordinate indexes. If an index of lesser depth is required, there is still another possibility, the keyword from title index, which will be discussed in the next chapter.

REFERENCES

1. Taylor, H., *Selective Device*. U.S. Patent 1,165,465, December 28, 1915.
2. National Science Foundation, *Nonconventional Scientific and Technical Information Systems in Current Use,* Number 4, National Science Foundation, 1966.
3. Cushing, R., "Improving Personal Filing Systems," *Chemical Engineering,* 70:73–86 (1963).
4. Wilkinson, W. A., "Indexing a Personal Reference File," *Special Libraries,* 50:16–18 (1959).
5. Cave, R., "A Method of Subject Indexing for the Private Library," *PLA Quarterly,* 1(6):69–73 (May 1958).
6. Gull, C. D., "Posting for the Uniterm System of Coordinate Indexing," *American Documentation,* 7:9–21 (1956).
7. Batten, W. E., "Specialized Files for Patent Searching," in *Punched Cards. Their Applications to Science and Industry,* R. S. Casey and J. W. Perry, eds. New York: Reinhold, 1951, pp. 169–181.
8. Starker, L. N. and Cordero, J. A., "A Multi-Level Retrieval System. I. A Simple Optical Coincidence Card System," *Journal of Chemical Documentation,* 8:81–85 (1968).

9. Mount, E., "Information Retrieval from Technical Reports Using Termatrex Equipment," *Special Libraries,* **54**:84–89 (1963).
10. Gull, *loc. cit.*
11. Linder, L. H., "Indexing Costs for 10,000 Documents," *Proceedings of the 1963 Annual Meeting of the American Documentation Institute,* Volume 2, pp. 147–148.
12. Mount, *op. cit.*, p. 89.
13. Jahoda, G., "Indexing with Edge-Notched and Internally Punched Cards," in *Information Retrieval Today,* W. Simonton, ed. Minneapolis, Minn.: U. of Minnesota Center for Continuation Study, 1963, p. 43.
14. Bourne, C. P., *Methods of Information Handling,* New York: John Wiley, 1963, pp. 57–68.
15. Mooers, C. N., "Zatocoding and Developments in Information Retrieval," *Aslib Proceedings,* **8**:6–8 (1956).
16. Batten, W. E., *op. cit.*, or *Punched Cards. Their Applications to Science and Industry,* 2nd ed., R. S. Casey, J. W. Perry, M. M. Berry and A. Kent, eds. New York: Reinhold, 1958.
17. Milne, L. J. and Milne, M., "Foresight and Hindsight on a Punch Card Bibliography," *American Documentation,* **10**:78–84 (1959).
18. Hinde, P. T., "Using Edge-Notched Cards for Personal Interest Literature Files," *Journal of Chemical Education,* **42**:565–569 (1965).
19. Hoff, W. I., "A Retrieval System for Health Education Information," *International Journal of Health Education,* **9**:87–93 (1966).
20. Harris, W. E. and Wallace, W. J., "A Bibliographic Punched Card in Analytical and Inorganic Chemistry Designed for the Individual Research Chemist," *Journal of Chemical Documentation,* **1**(3):36–53 (1961).
21. Thoma, J. A., "Simple and Rapid Method for the Coding of Punched Cards," *Science,* **137**:278–279 (July 1962).
22. Jahoda, *op. cit.*, p. 41.
23. Rees, T. H., "Commercially Available Equipment and Supplies," in *Punched Cards. Their Applications to Science and Industry,* 2nd ed., R. S. Casey, J. W. Perry, M. M. Berry and A. Kent, eds. New York: Reinhold, 1958, p. 32.
24. Begun, G. M., "Making Your Own Punched Cards," *Journal of Chemical Education,* **32**:328 (1955).

Chapter Six

Keyword-from-Title Indexes

About ten years ago an index based on words in titles of documents, and one that could be prepared with the aid of data processing equipment, was first publicly introduced. We now know that a keyword-from-title index prepared with the aid of data processing equipment has, in fact, been used by the Central Intelligence Agency since 1952, and that other such indexes not prepared with the aid of data processing equipment have been used for over 100 years.[1] While there is still some debate as to who started the whole system, evidence exists that keyword-from-title indexes have been used for a number of document collections. The format, first date of issue, and computer used for the preparation of 30 such indexes is given in a review by Stephens.[2] While a number of abstracting and indexing services, as well as libraries, have prepared and continue to prepare keyword-from-title indexes, we do not know too much about how successful these indexes are. In this respect, keyword-from-title indexes do not differ from other indexes. Some users proclaim that the keyword-from-title index is one of the best things that ever came along. Others feel considerably less kindly toward it. In this chapter we deal with techniques of index preparation, mention some of the variables that have been introduced, and conclude with a discussion of advantages and disadvantages of such indexes for personal document collections.

Keyword-from-title indexes are variously called permuted title indexes, keyword-in-context indexes or its acronym KWIC indexes, keyword-out-of-context indexes or its acronym KWOC indexes and, by those who are less than enthusiastic about them, the quick and dirty indexes. The individual unit or entry of a keyword-from-title index consists of an access point, the title of the document or a portion thereof, and the document identification code. The access point is a word or a phrase taken from the title. It may also be the name of the author of the document or a word that is not in the title, as we shall see.

Let us begin the discussion of this index with a description of a generalized procedure for its preparation. We will assume that the index is prepared without the aid of data processing equipment, although more often than not, this will not be the case. We have a collection of documents to be indexed. These documents have each been given a unique code for identification. Also, we made a list of words that are useless as access points because they carry little or no message, for example, articles and prepositions. The list of these words is called the delete word list since these words are eliminated as access points. We start the index process by looking at the title of the first document to be indexed. The first word in the title is checked against our delete word list. If the first title word is on the delete word list, we go to the next title word and repeat the matching process. Each title word that is not on the delete word list is made into an access point. The access point with either the entire title or part of the title surrounding the access point (given in context) and the document code constitute an entry for a document. One card is typed for each entry and the cards for a given document collection are arranged alphabetically by access point, which in this index is placed in the center of the line rather than in the left-hand margin. This would probably be the last step in index preparation of a pure and unrefined keyword-from-title index for a personal document collection. There is an advantage of having the index in book, rather than card, form. It is easier to scan the index in book form because one can look at several entries at one time. However, if only a single copy of the index is needed, as is likely to be the case for a personal index, retyping or photographing the entries to get the index in book form seems hard to justify. This procedure was described to give the reader a general idea as to how keyword-from-title indexes are prepared. The procedure is not recommended because most of the steps that we have just listed can be done more efficiently by computers if we give the machines specific instructions on what to do. Such instructions or computer programs are available for several computers.[3] Let us assume that we have access to a computer for which a program for preparing a keyword from title index is available. The program description will specify in what form the computer is willing to accept the information to be processed. Obviously, the information must be in machinable form. It must also follow a specified card format. Computers are very exacting. We must follow the required card format to the letter or the program will not run. A single card out of sequence or a wrong character punched in a single column can bring the program to a dead stop, and result in what the computer programmers so descriptively call a fatal error. The program will probably allow us to characterize any word in the title as a delete word and may also have certain built-in delete words such as all single character words or numbers. We will have to prepare and then submit a list of additional delete words in a form that the machine can understand, as words punched in designated columns on tabulating cards. There are other possible options in the program but we will discuss these subsequently.

Let us assume that we have one deck of punched cards with the titles of documents to be indexed along with the required bibliographic data. This is our data deck. We have a second deck that instructs the machine what to do with the data deck and this is the program deck. We also have a third deck of cards which contains the delete words that we have chosen for the index. The three decks of cards are fed into the computer in designated order. If all is well, the computer will then go to work. It examines the first word in the first title given to it and determines whether or not it is a delete word. This is not done by any feat of magic. Words are recognized as groups of symbols between spaces or designated punctuation marks. Title words are recognized by being in a specified portion of the tabulating card or by being preceded by a symbol that characterizes the word as a title word. The first title word that is identified is compared against the delete word list. If the word is on the delete word list it is not to be made into an access point. All other words are made into access points. If the first title word is on the delete word list, the computer goes to the next title word, and the next after that until it finds a word that is not on the delete word list. This word, along with the rest of the title (or a specified portion thereof), and the document code is put into a temporary storage area in the computer for subsequent sorting. The procedure is repeated for all words in the first title and then followed one title after another until the computer has in its temporary storage area a list of access points (non-delete title words) with corresponding title (or portion of title) and document code for all documents to be included in the index. When the machine has such a list of entries, the entries are alphabetized and the computer is now ready to print out the final version of the index on sheets of paper.

The printout can then be separated into pages and inserted between covers and then becomes the keyword-from-title index, or it can be photographed and reduced in size to yield a less bulky product. The latter option is usually taken when six or more copies of an index are needed. When more than six copies are needed, the printout can be prepared on a duplicating master (offset, mimeograph, hectograph). If a photographic process is used, the original printout can be reduced in size. A reduction to 47.4% of the original size of the printout fits a standard $8\frac{1}{2}'' \times 11''$ page. This is about the maximum reduction suggested. In fact, even this reduction results in an index that is difficult to read for some index users.

The described steps are something of an oversimplification and are not intended as specific instructions for the computer. In fact, some steps, such as the automatic generation of the document code based on the author's name, the date, the title, and the preparation of an author index, have been omitted altogether in this description. For a fuller description of how a computer prepares a keyword-from-title index, the reader is referred to an article by Kennedy.[4]

Searching a keyword-from-title index is, paradoxically, both a simple and a complex matter. It is simple because searching consists of looking under selected access points that are arranged alphabetically in the index and selecting documents that look potentially relevant with relevance judgments being based on the information given in the title. Searching is complex because most keyword-from-title indexes do not have elements of vocabulary control and this makes it a difficult task to select the access points in the index that might lead one to potentially relevant documents.

Some of the options that are available on at least some of the keyword-from-title indexes will now be mentioned. Hans Peter Luhn was one of the first to prepare keyword-from-title indexes with the aid of data processing equipment. He also coined the term "KWIC index."[5] Luhn's KWIC index consists of entries each occupying one line of 60 or fewer characters, including blank spaces. The access point is listed in the center of the page, surrounded by the words in the title in their original order, the context of the keyword, hence the name keyword-in-context index. The original Luhn index had very few delete words. Only the following words in titles were deleted as access points: a, an, and, as, at, by, for, from, if, in, of, on, or, the, to, with. Luhn reasoned that even this small number of delete words results in a substantial reduction in the number of access points. It is better, he argued, to have the index user skip any other nondesirable access points (which can be done quickly) than to omit words that might be useful to index users. A portion of a KWIC index and the bibliography for the index is reproduced as Figure 6-1. Notice that only a part of the title is given for lengthy titles, specifically titles that occupy more than a line of 60 characters. Also notice that when title words have to be chopped off at the right of the access point and when there is space to the left of the access point, part of the title is shifted from the right to the left of the access point. The full bibliographic citation is not given with each entry. The index user, is, therefore, forced to identify selected documents in the bibliography which is a listing of the indexed documents by order of the document code. Some document titles are less than informative and when this is the case, titles can be modified or rewritten. The computer does not care what words are used in the title as long as no more space is used than is provided for this purpose. With a 60-character line, some titles cannot be included in full. Some keyword-from-title indexes have, therefore, used a wider line for a title or even several lines per title. The filing of the access point in the center of the index line pleased some index users but displeased others. For the latter group of users, the access point was placed where it is located in other indexes, on the left margin of the page. This became a keyword-out-of-context index and was therefore called the KWOC index. An excerpt of a KWOC index is illustrated in Figure 6-2. Notice that in this index the keyword is followed by the entire title and that several lines are used per entry. Some KWOC indexes have the option of interfiling author names with keywords from titles, other KWOC indexes have separate author and title word sections.

The document code also enjoyed the attention of keyword-from-title index designers. In its simplest form, the document code is a unique accession number that also gives the physical location of the document. Luhn went a step further and programmed the computer to generate a unique code for each document that is included in the index and this code now bears Luhn's name. The computer-generated Luhn code consists of 11 characters. Six of the characters are letters of the author's last name, first name, and middle initial, 2 are for the decade and year of publication, and 3 are for the initials of the first 3 significant words in the title (title words that are not delete words). The Luhn code is used in the excerpt of the KWIC index reproduced as Figure 6-1. The Luhn code results in an alphabetic arrangement of the entries in the bibliography by name of first author with a sub-arrangement by date. Another arrangement of the bibliography is obtained by assigning each indexed document a unique code based on its method of filing in a subject folder. A one- or two-letter code may be assigned to each subject file folder. Each document in the file folder is then given a unique serial number for that file folder. The listing of documents by their code (one or two letters plus number) is thus an exact listing of their filing arrangement, or in the parlance of librarianship, a shelf list.

Variations are also possible in the physical makeup of the index. We have already mentioned the possibility of photo-reducing the print-out of the index that comes from the computer as a means of making it a more portable and easier-to-scan product. Access points in KWIC indexes can be highlighted and therefore made easier to see by shading the area on the page to the left of the access points.

A keyword-from-title index printed from a computer that has upper case typeface only and a standard set of characters lacks symbols such as colons, semi-colons, exclamation points, and other typographic niceties as exemplified by bold print, underlining, non-Roman alphabet characters, diacritical marks, subscripted and superscripted numerals. An editing step is therefore necessary (or at least highly desirable) to compensate for the missing type characters. In chemistry, for example, some abbreviations have to be spelled out to avoid ambiguity. CO can stand for either carbon monoxide or for Co, the element Cobalt. To indicate which of these meanings applies, the abbreviations have to be spelled out. Greek letters have to be represented as either letters of the Roman alphabet, or if this causes confusion, the letters have to be spelled out. These are some of the editing steps that are suggested before the index preparation can be turned over to a keypuncher and then the computer. There are other editing steps that should be considered. Foreign language titles should be translated into English. Sometimes word pairs are best kept together as access points since they become relatively meaningless as separate words. This can be done as one of the options of some of the computer programs. For example, if the phrase "free energy" is to be kept together as an access point instead of being split into two access points, some computer programs allow one to do so by adding a hyphen between words that are to be kept together. The amount of editing that is done on document titles represents another variable in keyword-from-title indexes.

The present writer has been involved in the preparation of several keyword-from-title indexes to researchers' document collections. Researchers in the sciences and engineering at Florida State University who told us that they have made extensive use of their document collections (one or more times per day) and who were unhappy with the way the documents had to be searched were invited to participate in an indexing study. The study was started by asking the participating researchers to collect case histories of subject uses of their document collections. A case history of a subject use consisted of a record of

```
     OSYNTACTIC RESEARCH.= SLAVIC LANGUAGES - COMPARATIVE MORPH   PACAM -63-SLC
RS AND DISCUSSION.= THE   SLIC INDEX. LOOKING FORWARD IN DOCUM   SHARJR-65-SIL
ONTROL AND STORAGE OF A   SLIDE FILE COLLECTION.= C              DAVIB -56-CSS
UT SYSTEM.= TMCL-- 70MM   SLIDE RETRIEVAL, DISPLAY AND PRINT-O   RYDEJP-65-T7S
H CARD FILE SYSTEM (FOR   SLIDES AND NEGATIVES).= PUNC           DAVILR-53-PCF
 FILING SYSTEM FOR YOUR   SLIDES.= PUNCH CARD                    PATTAR-50-PCF
   BOOK CATALOGS.= BOEING  SLIP.● COMPUTER PRODUCED AND MAINTAI  WEINEA-63-BSC
PERIENCES IN THE USE OF   SLIT PUNCHED CARDS IN THE ZENTRALE-K   LOSEI -62-EUS
OLES, PUNCHES, NOTCHES,   SLOTS AND LOGIC.= H                    GULLCD-58-HPN
RY FOR THE LABORATORY.=   SLOTTED PUNCH-CARDS OF ORGANIC CHEMI   ZIEGHJ-65-SPO
ITS OF MECHANIZATION IN   SMALL APPLICATIONS.= LIM               SCHUCK-59-LMS
 O CHARGING SYSTEM FOR A  SMALL COLLEGE LIBRARY.= PUNCHED- CAR   HOCKML-57-PCC
UTTING THE CATALOG OF A   SMALL COMPANY LIBRARY INTO THE KWIC    LAUBAF-64-PCS
NFORMATION CENTER FOR A   SMALL ENGINEERING DEPARTMENT.= DEVEL   BOLLWL-63-DSI
ATION OF AN INDEX FOR A   SMALL FILE.= RAPID STRUCTURE SEARCHE   GRANC -65-RSS
STEMS OF INFORMATION IN   SMALL GROUP RESEARCH STUDIES.= SY      MCGRJE-62-SIS
MENT.= DEVELOPMENT OF A   SMALL INFORMATION CENTER FOR A SMALL   BOLLWL-63-DSI
ROGRESS AND GROWTH OF A   SMALL MANUAL SYSTEM.= COORDINATE IND   CLARGM-62-CIP
FTWARE FOR AUTOMATING A   SMALL METALS RESEARCH REPORT COLLECT   GIBSE -65-KSA
NFORMATION STORAGE WITH   SMALL REDUNDANCY.= /GERMAN/ I          FEITW -65-ISS
ORMATION RETRIEVAL ON A   SMALL TO MEDIUM SIZE COMPUTER.= A FL   OLMEJ -63-FDF
           YSTEMS.= SMALL- SCALE INFORMATION RETRIEVAL S         WALLE -62-SSI
OF CONGRESS.= ROLE OF A   SMALL-SCALE COMPUTER UNDER STUDY AT    LIRRJO-62-RSC
RMATION RETRIEVAL USING   SMALL-SCALE MACHINES.= NEW METHODS F   PEPIR -60-NMM
ORGANIC STRUCTURES FROM   SMALL-TO-MEDIUM SIZED COLLECTIONS.=    BARNAJ-65-RIO
           TIME/ SYSTEM.= SMART / SOCONY MOBILE AUTOMATIC REAL   COOPRL-65-SSM
--AN ILLUSTRATION.= THE   SMART AUTOMATIC DOCUMENT RETRIEVAL S   SALTG -65-SAD
 RETRIEVAL SYSTEM.= THE   SMART AUTOMATIC TEXT PROCESSING AND    LESKM -64-SAT
              A SMART     SMART CLUSTERING PROGRAM.=             PRIVA -65-SCP
        THE EXTENDED      SMART SYSTEM.=                         EVSLT -64-ESS
DESCRIPTION OF THE NEW    SMART SYSTEM.= A SPECIFIC              EVSLT -65-SDN
RESULTS IN THE EXTENDED   SMART SYSTEM.= EVALUATION OF RETRIEV   LESKM -65-ERR
ON INPUT TO THE REVISED   SMART SYSTEM.= SPECIFICATI             LESKM -65-SIR
MPLETE SENTENCES IN THE   SMART SYSTEM.= SYNTACTIC ANALYSIS OF   PROWJ -65-SAI
TEST RESULTS USING THE    SMART SYSTEM.= THE EVALUATION OF AUT   SALTG -64-EAR
            ENCE.= THE    SMART SYSTEM-TYPICAL PROCESSING SEQU   LESKM -64-SSP
A PROGRESS REPORT ON      SMART.=                                SALTG -65-PRS
YNTACTIC PROCESSING FOR   SMART.= THE REVISED S                  LEMMA -65-RSP
S ON THE APPLICATION TO   SOCIAL SCIENCE MATERIAL OF UP-TO-DAT   KYLEB -58-SFC
UTED TITLE INDEX IN THE   SOCIAL SCIENCES AND THE HUMANITIES.=   FARLE -63-NPT
AL SYSTEM INITIATED FOR   SOCIAL SCIENCES.= COMPUTERIZED RETRI   LIBRJO-65-CRS
MATION RETRIEVAL IN THE   SOCIAL SCIENCES.= INFOR                FOSKDJ-64-IRS
S OF VERBAL DATA IN THE   SOCIAL SCIENCES.= THE GENERAL INQUIR   DUNPDC-65-GIF
TOWARD AN INTERNATIONAL   SOCIAL WELFARE DOCUMENTS SYSTEM.=      HOFFJR-65-TIS
ARD SYSTEM FOR INDEXING   SOCIAL WELFARE PUBLICATIONS.= MANUAL   HOFFJR-61-MHP
ROLE OF THE ENGINEERING   SOCIETIES IN A NATIONAL INFORMATION    COTTNE-65-RES
  INFORMATION PROCESSING  SOCIETIES/.= THEIR OWN DEVICES. /REP   KENTA -62-TOD
OLOGY WITHIN THE GERMAN   SOCIETY FOR DOCUMENTATION.= / PUNCHE   SCHEM -58-ERC
MENTATION AT THE GERMAN   SOCIETY FOR DOCUMENTATION.= /GERMAN/   MEYEKH-62-SRA
REPORT OF THE AMERICAN    SOCIETY FOR METALS LITERATURE SEARCH   KENTA -57-ALR
NTATION OF THE AMERICAN   SOCIETY FOR METALS MARK II DOCUMENTA   SHEPCA-64-DIA
  INFORMATION NEEDS OF    SOCIETY WITH RESPECT TO THE AREA OF    ROSEM -65-INS
CIENCE FOR THE NEEDS OF   SOCIETY.= INFORMATION SYSTEMS - ESSE   EJC AA-62-ISE
IC INFORMATION NEEDS OF   SOCIETY.= SCIENTIF                     AUGEP -65-SIN
 .= CITATION INDEXES IN   SOCIOLOGICAL AND HISTORICAL RESEARCH   GARFE -63-CIS
OME BIBLIOGRAPHICAL AND   SOCIOLOGICAL DEVICES TO IMPROVE MAIN   FLOOMM-65-SBS
          YSTEM.= SMART / SOCONY MOBILE AUTOMATIC REAL TIME/ S   COOPRL-65-SSM
ORT COLLECTION.= KWIC--   SOFTWARE FOR AUTOMATING A SMALL META   GIBSE -65-KSA
OF CRYSTALLOGRAPHY AND    SOLID STATE PHYSICS.= SCIENTIFIC INF   WATAT -62-SIF
ORGANIC COMPOUNDS. ONE    SOLUTION AMONG HUNDREDS.= HANDLING O   JANNEA-65-HOC
REPRODUCTION.● PERFECT    SOLUTION FOR SHORT RUNS.= FLEXOWRITE   WITTFJ-57-FCC
       PROBLEM.= ON THE   SOLUTION OF AN INFORMATION RETRIEVAL   SAMSBH-63-SIR
ROLS ALLOYS.= AUTOMATIC   SOLUTION OF DOCUMENTATION PROBLEMS,    SCHNK -61-ASD
       OBSOLESCENCE.$=    SOLUTION TO INFORMATION PROBLEMS OR    KONEEB-65-SIP
        L PROBLEM.= A     SOLUTION TO THE INFORMATION RETRIEVA   HOLMBE-62-SIR
CHEMICAL LITERATURE.= A   SOLUTION TO THE PROBLEM OF STORAGE A   WILLTJ-52-SPS
COORDINATE INDEXING - A   SOLUTION.= INFORMATION RETRIEVAL - T   HOLMBE-65-IRP
```

Figure 6-1. Excerpt from keyword-in-context index and bibliography for index. (*Literature on Information Retrieval and Machine Translation*, 2nd ed., C. F. Balz and R. H. Stanwood, IBM Corp., 1966.)

ERIKA -63-DRM   ERIKSON A
                 DOCUMENT RETRIEVER MATCHES POSITIVE AND NEGATIVE IMAGES.=
                 CONTROL ENGINEERING,JANUARY 1963,10,NO.1,127-9.
ERNSHA-59-DEL   ERNST HA
                 DESIGN AND EVALUATION OF A LITERATURE RETRIEVAL SCHEME.=
                 MASSACHUSETTS INSTITUTE OF TECHNOLOGY,CAMBRIDGE,MASS.,
                 M.S.THESIS,1959,73P.
ERNSML-64-EPL   ERNST ML
                 EVALUATION OF PERFORMANCE OF LARGE INFORMATION RETRIEVAL
                 SYSTEMS.=
                 CONGRESS ON THE INFORMATION SYSTEM SCIENCES,2D,HOT
                 SPRINGS,VA.,NOVEMBER 22-25,1964.,PREPRINTS,131-44.,
                 SESSION 7.• INFORMATION SYSTEM ANALYSIS.,PROCEEDINGS,
                 239-49.
ERNSML-65-CD   ERNST ML   GIULIANO VE   JONES PE
                 CENTRALIZATION AND DOCUMENTATION.=   /LETTER/
                 COMMUNICATIONS OF THE ACM,8,NO.11,NOVEMBER 1965,704-6,710
ERSHAP-58-ATU   ERSHOV AP
                 AUTOMATIC TRANSLATION IN THE USSR.=
                 MECHANIZATION OF THOUGHT PROCESSES SYMPOSIUM PROCEEDINGS,
                 NATIONAL PHYSICAL LABORATORY,TEDDINGTON,ENGLAND,1958.
                 351-4.
ERSKPL-63-CIB   ERSKINE PL
                 CO-ORDINATE INDEXING.=   / BIBLIOGRAPHY/
                 ASLIB PROCEEDINGS,FEBRUARY 1963,15,NO.2,41-61.
EVANLH-62-AIR   EVANS LH
                 ABC/S OF INFORMATION RETRIEVAL.=
                 AUDIOVISUAL INSTRUCTION,JANUARY 1962,7,28-9.
EVENPR-63-CCA   EVENING PRESS
                 COMPUTER CHALLENGES AUTHORSHIP OF ST. PAUL LETTERS.=
                 / LITERARY-DATA-PROCESSING/
                 THE EVENING PRESS,BINGHAMTON,NY,NOVEMBER 21,1963,18.
EVENPR-63-TMN   EVENING PRESS
                 TRANSLATIONS BY MACHINE NEAR.=
                 THE EVENING PRESS,BINGHAMTON,NY,OCTOBER 16,1963,3.
EVEYRJ-63-TAP   EVEY RJ
                 THE THEORY AND APPLICATIONS OF PUSHDOWN STORE MACHINES.=
                 HARVARD UNIVERSITY,CAMBRIDGE,MASS.,PB-163268,MAY 1963,
                 236P.
EVSLT -64-ESS   EVSLIN T
                 THE EXTENDED SMART SYSTEM.=
                 HARVARD UNIVERSITY, COMPUTATION LABORATORY. INFORMATION
                 STORAGE AND RETRIEVAL,CAMBRIDGE,MASS.,SCIENTIFIC REPORT
                 NO. ISR-8, DECEMBER 1964, SEC. 8, 18P.
EVSLT -65-SDN   EVSLIN T
                 A SPECIFIC DESCRIPTION OF THE NEW SMART SYSTEM.=
                 HARVARD UNIVERSITY,COMPUTATION LABORATORY,INFORMATION
                 STORAGE AND RETRIEVAL,CAMBRIDGE,MASS.,AUGUST 1965,
                 SECTION3,SCIENTIFIC REPORT NO. ISR-9,21P.
EVSLT -65-VMV   EVSLIN T   HOCHGESANG G   LESK M
                 VECTOR MERGING AND VECTOR CORRELATIONS.=
                 HARVARD UNIVERSITY,COMPUTATION LABORATORY,INFORMATION
                 STORAGE AND RETRIEVAL,CAMBRIDGE,MASS.,AUGUST 1965,
                 SECTION 13,SCIENTIFIC REPORT NO. ISR-9,26P.
FAIES -63-UPI   FAIELLO S
                 THE UNSOLVED PROBLEMS OF INFORMATION RETRIEVAL.=
                 SYSTEMS MANAGEMENT,MARCH-APRIL 1963,4,NO.2,30,38,40.
FAIES -63-VBI   FAIELLO S
                 VAST BUSINESS OF INFORMATION.=
                 NEW JERSEY BUSINESS,APRIL 1963,9,30-2.
FAIREM-36-IBW   FAIR EM
                 INVENTIONS AND BOOKS - WHAT OF THE FUTURES.=
                 LIBRARY JOURNAL,JANUARY 15,1936,61,NO.2,47-51.
FAIRRA-54-NNC   FAIRTHORNE RA
                 NOTES ON THE NLL CARD CATALOGUE OF AERODYNAMIC
                 MEASUREMENTS.=
                 JOURNAL OF DOCUMENTATION,1954,10,NO.1,11-18.

Figure 6-1.   (*Continued*)

METHYLPLATINUM(II)   ALKYLS AND ARYLS OF TRANSITION-METALS (PART-II) COMPLEX METHYLPLATINUM(III) DERIVATIVES   F-060
ADD ZZF-060*   CHATT-J * SHAW-B L
J CHEM SUC 705-16 (1959)   53-13991D

METHYLSULFIDE   SOME SUBSTITUTED METAL-CARBONYLS WITH LIGANDS HAVING SULFUR AS THE DONOR ATOM *ADD*   D-014
MOLYBDENUM* METHYLSULFIDE* THIOPHENE* THIOACETAMIDE* TROPYLIDENE* CYCLOHEXATRIENE*
ZZD-014*   COTTON-F A * ZINGALES-F
CHEM AND IND 1219 (1960)   55-13154B

METHYLTRIFLUOROMETHY   PHOSPHINES CONTAINING THE METHYLTRIFLUOROMETHYLPHOSPHINE GROUP *ADD* FLUOROPHOSPHINE*   A-059
ZZA-059*   BURG-A B * JOSHI-K K * NIXON-J F
JACS 88(1) 31 (1966)   64-5128E

METHYL-DERIVATIVE   METHYL-DERIVATIVE OF COBALT-CARBONYL-HYDRIDE *ADD* ZZE-015*   HIEBER-W * VOHLER-O *   E-015
BRAUN-G
Z NATURFORSCH 13B 192 (1958)   52-17092E

METHYL(2)-1,3-BUTADI   INFRARED AND NUCLEAR-MAGNETIC-RESONANCE STUDIES OF SOME PI-ALLYL TYPE COMPLEXES *ADD*   E-052
CARBONYL* HYDRIDE* COBALT* BUTADIENE(1,3)* METHYL(2)-1,3-BUTADIENE* PENTADIENE(1,3)*
PENTADIENE(1,4)* DIMETHYL(2,3)-1,3-BUTADIENE* ZZE-052*   BERTRAND-J A * JONASSEN-H B
* MOORE-D W

METHYL(4)-TRIOXAI2-6   TRANSITION-METAL COMPLEXES OF A CONSTRAINED PHOSPHITE ESTER (III) METAL CARBONYL   D-122
COMPLEXES OF METHYL(4)-TRIOXA(2-6-7)-PHOSPHABICYCLO(1)-OCTANE(2-2-2) *ADD* ZZD-122*
VERKADE-J G * MCCARLEY-R E * HENDRICKER-D G * KING-R W
INORG CHEM 4 228 (1965)   62-6121G

METHYPENTADIENYL-IRO   ORGANO IRON COMPLEXES (III) REACTIONS OF THE METHYPENTADIENYL-IRON TRICARBONYL CATION   E-167
ADD ZZE-167*   MAHLER-J E * GIBSON-D E * PETTIT-R
JACS 85 3959 (1963)

METLIN-S   BEHAVIOR OF DICOBALT-OCTOCARBONYL AT ELEVATED TEMPERATURE AND CARBON-MONOXIDE PRESSURE   D-027
ADD COBALT* ZZD-027*   METLIN-S * WENDER-I * STERNBERG-H W
NATURE 183 457-58 (1959)

KINETICS AND MECHANISM OF THE HYDROFORMYLATION REACTION   THE EFFECT OF OLEFIN STRUCTURE   I-006
ON RATE *ADD* ZZI-006*   WENDER-I * METLIN-S * ERGUN-S * STERNBERG-H W * GREENFIELD-H
JACS 78 5401-05 (1956)   51-2594F

Figure 6-2.   Excerpt from keyword-out-of-context index. (This is an index to the document collection of a researcher at Florida State University.)

the question and the citations of relevant documents that were selected for the question.* Twenty or more case histories of document use were collected from each researcher. The case histories were then analyzed to determine if a keyword-from-title index would be of potential interest to the researcher. Both the questions and the relevant document titles for each question were analyzed for concepts. The concepts in the question were compared with the concepts in relevant document titles to determine the extent of matching. Most keyword-from-title indexes are based on words in titles. If there is little coincidence between the words in the questions and the words in the title of relevant documents, or more abstractly, the concepts in the questions and the concepts in relevant document titles, then chances are that a keyword-from-title index is not likely to be useful. A concept in a question was said to match a concept in a title of a relevant document if the concepts were expressed by the same words, by synonyms, or at a different level of specificity. An example of concepts at different levels of specificity would be a question on glassware and a relevant document title that includes the word "beakers." An analysis of document collection use by six researchers (all of the researchers who participated in the project at that stage) indicated that at least one concept per question was matched by one concept in the title of each relevant document most (80 to 90%) of the time.

Keyword-from-title indexes were prepared for these six researchers and some of the details of index preparation are now discussed. The first step in the process was the assignment of a unique identifying code for each document to be included in the index. Since most of the documents were already filed in subject folders, a one- or two-letter code was assigned to each filing folder and the documents in each filing folder were given accession numbers. The unique code thus consists of a one- or two-letter code for the subject folder and a number to indicate filing sequence within the subject folder. Keyword-from-title index options were next discussed with the researcher. The CDC 6400 computer program that was used considered all 1-character symbols as delete words. All other delete words had to be specified by the researcher. A phrase could be made into a single access point by inserting a hyphen between the words in the phrase, for example, free-energy. Other editing options included the spelling out of ambiguous abbrevia-

---

* The problem of relevance is one that has been puzzling researchers in the field of index system design as well as researchers in other fields. This is because revelance is a subjective matter difficult to measure. The problem was sidestepped in this study by accepting the researcher's judgment of what he considered relevant for a given question.

tions, the translation of foreign titles into English, and the addition of words to the title words as access points.

Now for the mechanics of index preparation. The CDC 6400 computer program with the selected options required 5 tabulating cards per document to be included in the index. On these cards and in prescribed order were punched the name of the author or authors, the title of the document, added keywords to the title when used, the document code, the title of the journal, the volume and date of the journal, and page numbers or equivalent bibliographic information for other types of publications. The information to be keypunched per document was first transcribed onto a keypunch instruction form. The completed forms were then edited in accordance with the above-mentioned index options and the edited forms were used as keypunch instructions. The punched tabulating cards were then proofed and the necessary corrections were made. The 5 card decklet per document had to be fed into the computer in a prescribed sequence. No particular sequence of 5 card decklets for the documents was required. The 5 card decklets for the documents to be included in the index constitute the data deck.

The CDC 6400 prepares the KWOC index on magnetic tape. The magnetic tape was taken to the IBM 1401 computer which uses the tape to instruct the printer to print the index on a continuous form. The computer prepared the index on either a single or multiple copy continuous form. This form is separated into page-size sheets and when a multiple part form is used copies of the forms are separated. The index or indexes are inserted in binders. The computer-prepared index is in two parts: an alphabetic list of keyword and author entries and a listing of folder codes with document citations of documents filed under each folder. To these two parts is added an introduction that tells what documents are included in the index and the list of delete words used, and gives instructions for searching the index. The tabulating cards and/or the magnetic tapes for the index are saved for future updating of the index. A merge program is available to interfile into the index entries for newly received documents. First the magnetic tape is updated and then the magnetic tape is used to instruct the printer to print the updated index.

INDEX PREPARATION AND SEARCH TIME

The amount of time it takes to prepare a keyword-from-title index depends on the index options that are used as well as the computer that is used. The three principal time factors are clerical time, nonclerical time, and computer time. Index preparation times are now presented for the six keyword-out-of-context indexes that have just been described. Before giving these time figures, some of the parameters of the indexes are reviewed. The indexes lack vocabulary control. Keywords have been added to some titles by three out of six researchers but no record of how much nonclerical time this required is available. The indexes were prepared on the CDC 6400, a computer that is not particularly efficient for doing this, as we shall see when we compare time figures for index preparation with another computer. The index program that was used provides full titles with each access point—the keyword in the title, added keywords, and names of authors. This gives the index user considerable information with each access point but makes for a rather bulky index and one that takes longer to print than an index with fewer lines per indexed document. The personnel time for index preparation is given in Table 6-1.

Table 6-1
Personnel Time for Preparing a Keyword from Title Index

Clerical time		
Copying citations	16/hour	3.7 min./document
Keypunching	48/hour	1.25 min./document
Proofing	48/hour	1.25 min./document
Nonclerical time		
Editing	35/hour	1.7 min./document

The 6 to 7 minutes per document is probably a good estimate for clerical input time for a keyword-from-title index. The nonclerical time does not include the time taken by the researchers to add keywords to titles when they performed this task. (Not all of the researchers considered this step necessary.) Also, the nonclerical time can be close to nothing when no refinements are made in the index and the time can go to considerably more than 2 minutes if elements of vocabulary control and other refinements are added to the index. The central processing unit time on the CDC 6400 computer came to about 2.7 seconds per document. This is considerably higher than the 0.5 seconds per document figure reported by Kennedy for a slower computer, the IBM 7090 but one that is better suited for this operation.[6]

How long does it take to search a keyword-from-title index? Once again it depends on the type of question, the skill of the searcher, the attempted completeness of retrieval, and the available index options. In a series of test searches of keyword-out-of-context indexes to personal document collections in researchers' offices at Florida State University, the merged personal indexes of three chemists, search times were kept. Each index contained 3200 plus documents and was searched by 14 graduate chemistry students for questions that were previously searched by the chemists in their own document collections. The average search time per question per student was 18 minutes. The search time ranged from 7 to 51 minutes. It should be pointed out that the students were instructed to locate all of the relevant documents for a question. This probably is not a typical search request.

SUMMARY

Let us review some of the advantages and disadvantages of the keyword-from-title index and compare it with a coordinate index. If a computer with a keyword-from-title index program is available to the researcher, an unrefined keyword-from-title index can be prepared with little intellectual effort. Clerical time amounts to about 7 minutes per document as against about 5 minutes per document for a coordinate index. Some computer time will, of course, have to be included in the total cost of the index. For this investment one gets an index with an average of 4 to 6 keywords per title (depending on the length of the title and the length of the delete word list), an author index, and a bibliographic listing of the documents. The computer printout is likely to be in upper case typeface only and to lack some punctuation marks that we are usually accustomed to seeing. The typographic limitations of the index as well as the physical characteristics of the index should be placed in the negative column of our ledger. We do not know, however, how much of a demerit we can assign to these aspects of the index since we have no measure of how much it slows down the index user, or, what would be even more serious, whether it stops one from using the index when one should use it. What about the difference in searching a keyword-from-title index and a coordinate index? Once again, it is difficult to make a direct comparison. The keyword-from-title index does not permit coordinate searches because combinations of words selected at the time of indexing must be used in searching the index. The keyword-from-title index provides more information with the access point than does the coordinate index other than a coordinate index on edge-notched cards. One can therefore assume that the searcher who has a keyword and a title or portion of a title will be able to select or reject a document more rapidly than if he had only the keyword as he does in the case of the coordinate index. While this is probably so, this does not mean that searches are conducted more rapidly in a keyword-from-title index than in a coordinate index. In fact, there is some feeling (the word is chosen deliberately since we lack concrete evidence) that the opposite is the case. The searches conducted at Florida State University in the keyword-from-title indexes to about 3200 documents—searches that attempted to locate all of the documents on the subject that were included in the index—took an average of 18 minutes per search. We suspect that equivalent searches in a coordinate index would not have taken this long but we have not conducted such searches, nor have we specified depth of index, vocabulary control, and other variables in the coordinate index.

The question of the type of index and the index options that should be selected for a specified situation are treated in a later chapter. There is another type of index to be discussed and one that can be produced with a minimum of intellectual effort. This is the citation index and it is covered in the next chapter.

REFERENCES

1. Fischer, M., "The KWIC Index Concept: A Retrospective View," *American Documentation,* **17**:57–70 (1966).
2. Stephens, M. E., *Automatic Indexing: A State of the Art Report. NBS Monograph 91.* Washington, D.C.; National Bureau of Standards, 1965. pp. 49–53.
3. Descriptions of programs for two computers with instructions for recording bibliographic information into machinable form are given in the following two publications: Control Data Corporation, Application Development Bulletin, 6000 KWIC, Minneapolis, Minnesota (n.d.). IBM Corporation Keyword-in-Context (KWIC) Indexing Program, 1401-CR-02X, IBM 1401/1460 Program Library, IMB Data Processing Division, White Plains, New York, 1964.
4. Kennedy, R. A., "Library Applications of Permutation Indexing," *Journal of Chemical Documentation,* **2**:181–185 (1962).
5. Luhn, H. P., "Keyword in-Context Index for Technical Literature," *American Documentation,* **11**:288–295 (1960).
6. Kennedy, *op. cit.*, p. 184.

Chapter Seven

Citation Indexes

A commonly used technique of conducting a literature search is to begin the search with a relevant document and look up the references cited in this document. The rationale is that references cited in a paper of interest are likely to be on the same or a related subject and, therefore, also of interest. After all, when an author prepares an article on a subject he should tell his readers what others have done before him on this subject if only to indicate that he knows more. It might help in understanding what a citation index is all about if we look at Figure 7-1 and consider the references cited in the 1963 Swets paper as the ancestors of this paper. If we turn the analogy around, the paper becomes the descendant of the papers that were cited in it. If we look at the papers, or more broadly at the documents, cited in the 1963 Swets paper, we make a search that goes back in time. But it would be nice to be able to make a search forward in time, a search that would enable us to locate the descendants of the 1963 Swets paper. And this is exactly what we can do with a citation index. The citation index to a single paper, the 1963 Swets paper, is given in Figure 7-2. This is simply a list of the documents that cite Swets' 1963 article. The document ancestors are usually called the *cited* documents and the document descendants are usually called the *citing* documents. We too will use this

1. C. P. Bourne, G. D. Peterson, B. Lefkowitz, and D. Ford, *Stanford Res. Inst. Proj. Rept. No. 3741* (1961).
2. H. Bornstein, *Am. Doc.* **12**, 254 (1961).
3. R. E. Wyllys, *Trans. Congr. Inform. System Sci., Hot Springs, Va., 1st* (1962).
4. J. Verhoeff, W. Goffman, J. Belzer, *Commun. Assoc. Computing Machinery* **4**, 557 (1961).
5. D. R. Swanson, *Science* **132**, 1099 (1960).
6. H. Borko, *System Development Corp., Santa Monica, Calif., Field Note No. 5649/000/01* (1961).
7. C. N. Mooers, *Zator Company, Cambridge, Mass., Tech. Note No. RADC-TN-59-160* (1959).
8. J. W. Perry and A. Kent, Eds., *Tools for Machine Literature Searching* (Interscience, New York, 1958), pp. 3–18.
9. C. W. Cleverdon, *Association of Special Libraries and Information Bureaux, Cranfield, England, Interim Rept.* (1962).
10. D. R. Swanson, paper presented at the Congress of the International Federation of Information Processing Societies, Munich (1962).
11. M. E. Maron and J. L. Kuhns, *J. Assoc. Computing Machinery* **7**, 216 (1960).
12. H. M. Wordsworth and R. E. Booth, *Western Reserve Univ. Tech. Note No. 8, AFOSR-TN-59-418* (1959).
13. A. Wald, *Statistical Decision Functions* (Wiley, New York, 1950).
14. W. W. Peterson, T. G. Birdsall, W. C. Fox, *IRE (Inst. Radio Engrs.) Trans. Information Theory* **4**, 171 (1954); D. Van Meter and D. Middleton, *ibid.*, p. 119.
15. W. P. Tanner, Jr., and J. A. Swets, *Psychol. Rev.* **61**, 401 (1954); J. A. Swets, *Psychometrika* **26**, 49 (1961).
16. J. A. Swets, *Science* **134**, 168 (1961).

Figure 7-1. List of references cited in Swets, J. A. Information retrieval systems. *Science* **141**:245–50 (1963).

terminology. A citation index is thus a list of cited documents with the citing documents listed under each cited document.

Citation indexes are not a new idea. A citation index to the record of legal decisions, the Shepard Citation Index, was started in 1873. This index is still being published and is an indispensable tool to lawyers. A brief description of the Shepard Citation Index is given by Adair.[1] There are other citation indexes in the fields of statistics, radio engineering, and information science, and there is one that covers all areas of science.[2]

How citation indexes are used is now illustrated with an example. Let us assume we have heard of a new technique for evaluating indexes.

Cited Reference:

Swets, J. A., "Information Retrieval Systems," *Science* 141:245–250 (1963).

Citing References:

Brookes, B. C., "The Measures of Information Retrieval Effectiveness Proposed by Swets," *J. Doc.* 24:41–54 (1968).

Brownson, H. L., "Evaluation of Document Searching Systems and Procedures," *J. Doc.* 21:261–266 (1965).

Cooper, W. S., "Expected Search Length: A Single Measure of Retrieval Effectiveness Based on the Weak Ordering Action of Retrieval Systems," *Am. Doc.* 19:30–41 (1968).

Goffman, W. and Newell, V. A., "A Methodology for Testing and Evaluation of Information Retrieval Systems," *Infor. Stor. Retr.* 3:19–25 (1966).

King, D. W., "Evaluation of Coordinate Index Systems During File Development," *J. Chem. Doc.* 5:96–99 (1965).

Klempner, I. M., "Methodology for the Comparative Analysis of Information Storage and Retrieval Systems: A Critical Review," *Am. Doc.* 15:210–216 (1964).

Saracevic, T. and Rees, A. M., "Toward the Identification and Control of Variables in Information Retrieval Experimentation," *J. Doc.* 23:7–19 (1967).

Thornberry, H. H., "Symposium on Information Science. II. Progress in the Organization of an International Information Center on Photovirology, *Bact. Rev.* 29:516–522 (1965).

Figure 7-2. Example of citation index to a single cited reference.

This is a technique that was developed by Swets and published by him in *Science* in 1963, the article whose list of references is reproduced as Figure 7-1. We are interested in learning whether anyone has tested this technique and/or whether other researchers in this field have commented on it. This is a difficult search to conduct in subject indexes that we have discussed up to now, indexes that have to be approached by words—subject headings, descriptors, or keywords. The chances are that such subject indexes will not list relevant documents under the name of Swets' technique. The technique is not sufficiently established to warrant such treatment. A more general heading, index evaluation, is likely to yield a large number of documents with perhaps only a small portion of these documents mentioning the Swets technique. Researchers who have used the Swets technique or who are commenting on it are likely to refer to the Swets paper in their bibliography. Hence a citation index can be used to locate documents on this subject. In fact, the *Science Citation Index* (see references at the end of this chapter) was used to locate the citing documents listed in Figure 7-2. This was an example of a citation index search in which the cited document was known to the researcher when he started his search. Usually things are not quite so simple. One has to locate one or more documents on a subject as cited documents. Without a cited document one cannot begin a search of a citation index. It is, therefore, necessary to precede the search in the citation index with a search in a subject index that is approachable with a word or phrase unless, of course, we already know of such a document. Once the cited reference has been found, the first round of the citation index search can be made. As relevant citing documents are located, the search can be continued by making the citing document the cited document. For example, in Figure 7-2, the King 1965 paper is a citing paper. If papers citing the King paper are also of potential interest, the citation index search can be continued by looking under King's paper as the cited paper.

The preparation of a citation index to a researcher's document collection is now discussed. We do not use any mechanical device other than a typewriter for its preparation, although such indexes are usually prepared with the aid of data processing equipment. The citation index is prepared on index cards. Let us assume that each document to be included in the citation index (citing document) has a unique identifying code—either an accession number or a combination of letters and numbers to indicate filing location of the document. We begin by taking the first document that is to be included in the citation index and looking at its list of references (the cited documents). If the document has one or more cited references, an index card is prepared for each such reference. The cited reference is identified by bibliographic citation either in full or abbreviated form. The bibliographic citation of the cited document is typed on the top part of the card. Just below, we type the identifying code for the citing reference. The cards are filed by name of cited author or title for anonymous works. After we have prepared all of the cards for the first citing document we will continue the same procedure for subsequent citing documents except for one change. We can add more than one citing reference to a cited document card. The list of cited reference cards is therefore checked before a new cited reference card is made. When the indexing has been completed, we will have a deck of index cards arranged by author of cited references. On each card there will also be identifying codes of one or more citing documents. It is, of course, possible that a citing reference will also be a cited reference and thus appear in both roles. For example, the Swets 1963 article may be used both as a citing article and a cited article. Published citation indexes may also have a list of citing refer-ences, called the source (of citations) index. This is probably not neces-sary for an index to a personal document collection since the file of documents can serve this purpose.

Variables

As with other types of indexes that we have dealt with thus far, there are several options that come with citation indexes. One such option is the amount of information that is included per entry. An entry in the citation index is defined as a cited reference–citing reference com-bination. Let us first consider the amount of bibliographic information to be given per cited and citing reference. We can give the full biblio-graphic citation as we have done in Figure 7-2 and this makes for an index that is easier to use but bulkier and more expensive to prepare than one in which the bibliographic citation is condensed. In some early trials of citation indexing by Tukey, prepared at a time when no clerical help was available, the citation for a journal consisted of only the volume number, journal title, and beginning page, all in abbreviated form. Tukey has since expanded his citation by adding to the items above the year and decade of publication, a three-letter code for the first named author's last name, the closing page number, and a two-character multiple-pur-pose code.[3] The index entry can be made more informative in several ways as suggested by Lipetz. One can add keywords to the titles to give the searcher a better idea of what the document is all about. One can specify the type of document that is cited, whether it is a journal article, a review, a bibliography, a data compilation, or other type of publication. One can also indicate the relationship between the cited and citing documents. Example of such relationships might be affirma-tion, refutation, explanation, or improvement of the work reported in the cited document.[4] While all of these suggestions are of potential use to the searcher, they do add to the clerical and in some cases to the nonclerical time needed for preparing the index.

Another variable is the arrangement of the index entries. Tukey suggests three possibilities according to where the cited items appear. If it is a journal article, this would be by journal title; by full name or abbreviation of the first named author's name; by initial page number of the cited reference.[5] There is no evidence that one arrangement is superior to another. One also has the choice of making an index to all of the cited documents in a given collection or to only a selected portion thereof. The selection may be based on the type of publication cited. For example, one might only include citations that are journal articles or books and disregard reports and other ephemera as well as hard-to-locate documents. The decision depends on the importance of particular types of documents to a researcher. The problem of locating cited documents brings up another variable. Citations are at times incomplete and at times inaccurate. Should one check the citations before including them in the index or should one take one's chances of frustration when one uses the index? The economics of the operation will probably lead one to opt for the latter alternative. The index can be prepared manually and on cards as was described or it can be prepared with aid of data processing equipment and in book form. There are no comparable cost studies available for these two alternative ways of citation index preparation. The index on cards does have the advantage of easy revision. Citations can be added to existing cards and/or newly prepared citation cards can be added to the file at any time. The citation index can be accompanied by a source-of-citations index, the list of citing documents. In the case of a citation index to a personal documents collection, the source-of-citation index does not have to be a separate list but can be the arrangement of documents on the shelves as was already pointed out. Other types of indexes can accompany the citation index and this possibility will be discussed in the next chapter.

Some Advantages and Disadvantages

A citation index, like a keyword-from-title index, may be prepared with little or no intellectual effort; and this is an advantage. In a very real sense, the author of a document will do the indexing for you since he connects his document to related documents and thus provides index entries for you. The author is in the best position to do this, if he takes the necessary time and effort. Some authors do not take this time and effort. The reasons are given by May: ". . . memory failures, lack of self-awareness, carelessness, plagiarism of other people's citations without having used them, the widespread custom of not citing 'obvious' sources and many other causes—all consequences of the simple fact that the author selects citations to serve his scientific, political, and personal goals and not to describe his intellectual ancestry."[6] The reader is left to decide whether this judgment of citation habits applies to authors in his field. If it does, a citation index is not likely to be attractive to him—even at a low cost. If it does not, the citation index has certain merits. It is not dependent on subjects expressed as subject headings, descriptors, and keywords, often false friends that have a tendency of lulling us into a false sense of security by making us believe that we have located everything on a subject even when this is not the case.

Citation indexes are not restricted to documents in one's collection—an advantage if one can get at the cited documents, a disadvantage if one cannot. The citation index must be approached with a cited document and the location of such a document may require the search of another index prior to one's being able to use a citation index.

Citation Indexes for Personal Document Collections

You will probably not want to consider a citation index to your document collection if either of the following two statements applies.

- The authors in your field are not particularly diligent about citing relevant documents.
- Your collection is too small to represent a useful portion of the cited literature.

There are not many reports of the use of citation indexes to personal document collections. Tukey writes about a citation index prepared by a researcher in the field of statistics. Each entry was recorded on a $3'' \times 5''$ index card. The only mechanization used was a toy rubber stamp (with movable type) to apply the citing item's designation. The code used was nonredundant and stressed compactness. When this, a wholly individually prepared citation index, had grown to fill about one moderately large desk drawer, it was already quite effective as a tool for statisticians.[7] Little information is available on the cost of preparing citation indexes. Lipetz writes that for a citation index prepared with the aid of unit record equipment, keypunching, proofing, editing, looking up, and correcting citations takes one hour of labor time for 15 cited references. To this time must be added sorting and printing time.[8] Garfield and Sher concluded that there are an average of 13.7 cited references per citing journal article in the field of science.[9] If we use this figure and the Lipetz figure for determining processing cost per citing document, we would come up with an input cost of about one hour per citing document. Chances are, however, that a major portion of the time given by Lipetz was for looking up and correcting cited references, something that we would probably not want to do. The actual time required would depend on the number of cited references per citing document and the amount of information to be recorded per entry. Once the average number of characters per entry has been determined, clerical costs can be approximated by looking at comparative costs for preparing keyword-from-title indexes. While we have been able to indicate circumstances when a citation index should not be used, we are not in a position to state specific circumstances under which a citation index should be used. The reader is advised to make some trial uses of one of the published citation indexes that are listed in the bibliography. This will help him to determine how useful such an index might be for his document collection. The use of a citation index in combination with other types of indexes is discussed in the next chapter.

REFERENCES

1. Adair, W. C., "Citation Indexes for Scientific Literature?" *American Documentation,* **6**:31–32 (1955).
2. The following are examples of published citation indexes: *Annals of Mathematical Statistics,* indexes to volumes 1–31, 1930–1960; Institute of Radio Engineers, *Transactions of the Professional Group on Information Theory,* annual index, 1958–   ; American Documentation Institute, *Automation and Scientific Communications,* index to short papers contributed to the theme session of the 26th annual meeting of the American Documentation Institute, 1963; The citation index that covers all the science is the *Science Citation Index* and it is published by the Institute for Scientific Information, Philadelphia, Pa.
3. Tukey, J. W., *The Citation Index and the Information Problem. Opportunities and Research in Progress.* 1962. Annual Report on National Science Foundation Grant, NSF-G-22108. Princeton Univ., n.d., pp. 31–32.
4. Lipetz, B. A., "Improvement of the Selectivity of Citation Indexes to Science Literature Through Inclusion of Citation Relationship Indicators," *American Documentation,* **16**:81–90 (1965).
5. Tukey, *op. cit.,* p. 34.
6. May, K. O., "Abuses of Citation Indexing," *Science,* **156**:890 (1967).
7. Tukey, *op. cit.,* p. 24.
8. Lipetz, B. A., "Compilation of an Experimental Citation Index from Scientific Literature," *American Documentation,* **13**:251–266 (1962).
9. Garfield, E. and Sher, I. H., "New Factors in the Evaluation of Scientific Literature Through Citation Indexes," *American Documentation,* **14**:195–201 (1963).

Chapter Eight

Other Indexes and Combination of Indexes

In this chapter we will discuss indexes that may be new to the reader. We will also reintroduce indexes that have been covered in previous chapters but we will talk about these indexes in a new role—their use in combination with each other.

KYPERCATSY

Barbara Kyle describes an index that is used for her personal document collection and that has the fanciful name of Kypercatsy. It is a unique index. Kypercatsy can be used for indexing books, correspondence, or other types of documents. Its application for the indexing of books will be described. The index is a record of readings with each reading recorded on a single line in a bound notebook. As a book is read for the first time, a serial number is assigned to it. If it belongs to the indexer, the book is also filed by the serial number. Each reading act is also given a serial number and this number plus the following information is recorded in the notebook: author, title and subtitle of book, personal relevance or reason for reading, date of use, serial number of book, serial numbers in notebook representing readings of books by the same author or by the same or related subjects. The last two items of information make this record more than a diary of readings. The record of related readings ties together in the index books by the same author or on the same or related subjects. Miss Kyle claims that the index has enabled her to answer questions that she has frequent occasion to ask and that could not be answered by other techniques. She claims that the system is geared to an individual's particular mental habits and that it points out relevant documents in the index with a minimum amount of effort on the part of the indexer-searcher. No cost figures are presented.[1]

FACETED CLASSIFICATION SYSTEMS

Faceted classification systems, like coordinate indexing systems, are systems based on concept coordination. Unlike coordinate indexes in which descriptors are combined at the time of searching to form the search heading, the index units of the faceted classification system are combined at the time of indexing. This is a difference between a precoordinate and a postcoordinate indexing system. The faceted classification system is a classification system since the index vocabulary is arranged in a logical order (by subject) rather than strictly alphabetic order. It differs from the hierarchically classified index that we have discussed in a previous chapter in that not all of the index headings for a given subject are listed (a characteristic of the enumerative classification system such as the Dewey Decimal Classification System). Instead, only the "building blocks" are listed and these are the concepts which when combined in specified ways become the index headings.

The selection of these "building blocks" and their arrangement in a logical order is a key part in the preparation of a faceted classification system. One of the first steps in the preparation of such a system is the selection of a small number of broad categories, say about a dozen or fewer, for a given area of interest. It should be pointed out that the faceted classification system is used for specialized fields rather than for all areas of knowledge and this is one reason why it is potentially applicable as an index to researchers' document collections. The broad categories into which a given subject is divided are called facets. Once the facets have been selected, the individual units or building blocks within each facet are selected. We will call these units the terms of the faceted classification system. It might be helpful to consider them to be similar to descriptors in a coordinate index although it should be remembered that in the faceted classification system the terms are combined to form the index heading at the time of indexing. An index heading with a document identification becomes an entry in the index. Several decisions need to be made in the design of a faceted classification system. These decisions include the following.

Decision on Order or Sequence of Facets. The combination of terms used to describe a document or an aspect thereof is listed to the index in only one place. The listing is based on an assigned sequence or priority order of facets. This assigned priority affects not only the access point of the entry (the first term in the entry) but also the order of the individual terms in the index heading. The assignment of facets order is based primarily on anticipated needs of the users.

Arrangement of List of Terms Within Each Facet. The individual terms within each facet can be arranged in several ways, with the decision again based on users' convenience. The arrangement may be by most important terms at the head of the list, by placing general headings before their subdivisions (a hierarchical arrangement), by strictly alphabetic arrangement, or by a combination of these arrangements.

Notation. A code is used to characterize each facet and each term within the facet. This is a space-saving device. The code for the term includes the code for the facet to which the term belongs. In the faceted classification schedule (the arrangement of terms under their facets) given in Figure 8-1, the facets are characterized by single capital letters, the terms under each facet as one or more lower case letters to which is added the capital letter for the corresponding facet. Some faceted classification systems use both letters and numbers in their notation.

Indication of Relationship Among Terms in an Index Heading. An index heading becomes more informative when terms are not only listed but when relationships among indexing terms are indicated. For this reason, the following types of relationships have been suggested: effect as, for example, the effect of physical structure on the engineering properties of a plastic; association without specific relationship specified as, for example, the growth *and* sexual maturity of aquatic mammals; comparison as, for example, Chemical A versus Chemical B as antioxidants; bias or study from a particular point of view as, for example, statistics for economics. The specified relationship is indicated by a punctuation mark or other symbol between the terms that are to be related.[2]

Container Manufacture: General	Facet A
Products	Facet B
Parts, Components	Facet C
Materials	Facet D
Operations	Facet F

FACET B

b	Metal containers
bb	Open-top cans
m	General line cans
r	Nonmetallic containers
s	Cartons
sz	Bottles
t	Flexible packages
v	Laminates

FACET C

b	Cylinders, bodies
c	Ends
h	Valves
q	Caps
qb	Screwcaps
v	Joints, seams

FACET D

b	Metals
c	Tinplate
d	Aluminum
g	Paper and board
k	Plastics
kc	Polythene
l	Film
q	Cork
qg	Glass
v	Coatings, decoration

FACET F

b	Analysis
c	Coating
d	Printing
f	Forming
fj	Extruding
fk	Impact extruding
fm	Moulding
g	Assembling
gc	Soldering
gt	Glueing
m	Testing, inspection
t	Coding
v	Storing

Figure 8-1. Faceted classification schedule for container manufacture.

Alphabetic Subject Index. Since each combination of terms is only listed once in the faceted classification system and since the entries are not in natural language but are represented as a shorthand notation, an alphabetic index to the terms and combination of terms is an essential part of a faceted classification system.

An excerpt of a faceted classification system in the field of container manufacture is given as Figure 8-1.[3] Let us illustrate the use of the system with the aid of an index entry and an alphabetic index that would lead a user to this entry. We have a document that can be indexed with terms listed in Figure 8-1. The document deals with the printing on plastic cartons. It is given a unique identifying code, number 1248 for example. The subject of the document is expressed by three terms: printing, plastic, and cartons. These terms are translated into their code, Fd, Dk, and Bs, respectively. The index entry for this document would be:

$$Bs: Dk: Fd—1248.$$

The terms are arranged in this order since terms listed in the B facet are filed before terms listed in the D facet which, in turn, are listed before terms in the F facet. This would be the only place in the index where this index heading for the document would be filed.

We need an alphabetic subject index to give us the code for a term that is to be searched in the faceted classification system. We also need the alphabetic subject index to tell us under what entry a term is to be found. A term may or may not be an access point in an entry. The alphabetic subject index enables us to find entries, whether or not the term under which we search the alphabetic subject index is an access point in the faceted classification system.

The three alphabetic subject index entries for the printing on plastic cartons entry would look like this:

> Cartons: see Bs
> Plastic: cartons   see Bs: Dk
> Printing: plastic: cartons   see Bs: Dk: Fd

Other applications of the faceted classification system include indexes in the fields of fine arts,[4] occupational safety and health,[5] food technology,[6] soil science,[7] and nuclear energy.[8]

There is no recorded description of the use of a faceted classification system for a researcher's personal document collection. We mention this index because we believe that its advantages merit consideration for use in personal document collections. The advantages of the system are:

• flexibility of design for specialized collections;
• characterization of subjects by means of a small number of terms;
• possibility of providing both specific and generic access points;
• possibility of indicating relationship among indexing terms.

A negative aspect of the system is the filing of groups of terms that characterize a document in one and only one place. Suggestions for getting around this disadvantage have been made. One can prepare a permuted term index and make each of the terms an access point as was done with the keyword-from-title index. One can also convert the faceted classification system into a coordinate index and thereby provide access points for each term or combination of terms. Tests on both of these modifications of the faceted classification system are reported by Vickery.[9]

AUTHOR INDEXES

Another type of index that has already been mentioned in passing is the author index. If one leafs through the pages of the science journals of 50 and more years ago, one notices the concern of scientists of those days with the problem of filing reprints, or authors' separates as they were then more commonly called. Much of the concern was with the size, composition and cost of the pamphlet boxes in which the documents were filed ($.10 per box was considered an exhorbitant price to pay). There was also concern about how to file the reprints. Here is what R. M. Harper had to say about the matter.

"It seems to be a common, if not the prevailing custom in private and semi-private scientific libraries to arrange pamphlets alphabetically by authors as Mr. Storer recommends. This has the advantage of obviating the mental exertion of classifying them by subjects (which ought to be an important consideration with that apparently increasing class of persons who prefer to follow a mechanical routine rather than exercise judgment) and of keeping together the writings of one's friends so that if a friend comes for a visit one can see at a glance just how many of his papers one has. But in most respects the alphabetical arrangement is an undesirable expedient."[10]

Mr. Harper is probably still correct in his conclusion about the inadequacy of author indexes as sole access points to a personal document collection. There are exceptions. One such exception would be a document collection on a subject in which there are few authors and one in which the authors can be associated with particular subjects. The researcher is likely to be interested in subjects and if the subjects can be approached through names of authors as was the case with the citation index, fine. Otherwise some type of subject index is desirable or even necessary. Author indexes can provide one type of access point in combination with other types of access points. And this brings us to the second part of the chapter, the discussion of combinations of indexes.

COMBINATIONS OF INDEXES

A combination of author and subject index is not uncommon. The reader is familiar with another combination index in libraries. This is the shelving of books by subject classification, which is one type of subject index, and the assignment of subject headings in the card catalog to these same books, which is another subject index. These two subject indexes complement each other. The classification system provides a relatively broad or generic approach to the book and is used as a means of shelving books so that books on related subjects are placed close to each other. The subject headings in the card catalog provide more specific access points for the books. A similar reasoning was followed in the discussion of the keyword-from-title index which was supplemented by filing of the indexed documents in subject folders. The keyword-from-title index provides relatively specific access points, the titles. The subject folders, on the other hand, are usually more generic and thus provide a different type of approach to the documents.

Tukey suggests more than two types of indexes to the same document collection and he calls his combination of indexes RECAP, an acronym derived for the names of the indexes. RECAP consists of the following four components.

1. Reference lists from articles (the bibliography at the end of articles).
2. Citation index.
3. Author index.
4. Permuted title index (a keyword-from-title index).

He believes that such indexes may not be practical for individual researchers but suggests that they might be provided for small groups of researchers working in the same field.[11]

Coordinate indexes can also be used in combination with other types of indexes. One such combination has already been mentioned in an earlier chapter. It is the preparation of a coordinate index, not to a single document but to a group of documents, that are filed in a subject folder. Again we have the generic approach through the subject heading folder and the specific approach through the coordinate index. This technique may be used for either part of the document collection or for the entire document collection but it is not without potential problems. If the coordinate index refers not to a single document but to a group of documents, chances of false drops increase. There is the possibility of false drops caused by coordinating descriptors that happen to be used for a document but that are not related to each other. To this possibility which occurs in all coordinate indexes we must add the possibility of false drops caused by indexing document folders rather than individual documents. If this turns out to be a problem (and this may well be so unless the subject folders contain only documents that should be indexed by the same descriptors), there is a way to get around it. One adds a unique code, say a letter for each document in the folder, and thus retrieves only specific documents when searching the coordinate index.

In the cases of the combination broad subject heading folder and either alphabetic subject index, coordinate index, or keyword-from-title index, a generic access point is added to the specific access points. The additional effort in doing this is not likely to be extensive. Documents have to be filed anyway and it takes little extra effort to file a document by subject rather than by accession number. The selection of a generic access point for each document is not likely to take more than a minute's time per document. The basic question is whether the generic access points are required. This and related questions that need to be answered in planning an index are discussed in the next chapter.

REFERENCES

1. Kyle, B., "Kypercatsy and Kypercorcon," Books; The Journal of the National Book League. No. 350:213–19 (1963).
2. Vickery, B. C., *Faceted Classification. A Guide to Construction and Use of Special Schemes.* London: Aslib, 1960, p. 37.
3. Foskett, D. J., "The Construction of a Faceted Classification for a Special Subject," *Proceedings of the International Conference on Scientific Information.* Washington, D.C.: National Academy of Sciences—National Research Council, 1959, pp. 886–887.
4. Broxis, P. F., "Faceted Classification and the Fine Arts," *Journal of Documentation,* 22:40–54 (1966).
5. Foskett, *op. cit.,* pp. 884–885.

6. Foskett, *op cit.,* p. 887.
7. Vickery, B. C., *Classification and Indexing in Science,* 2nd ed. London: Butterworths, 1959, pp. 195–203.
8. *Ibid.,* pp. 203–205.
9. Vickery, B. C., *Faceted Classification Schemes.* Graduate School of Library Service, Rutgers, the State University. New Brunswick, N.J., 1966, pp. 106–107.
10. Harper, R. M., "Suggestions for the Development of Scientific Libraries; with Special Reference to Authors' Separates," *Science,* 45:315 (1917).
11. Tukey, J. W., "Keeping Research in Contact with the Literature: Citation Indices and Beyond," *Journal of Chemical Documentation,* 2:34–37 (1962).

Chapter Nine

The Planning, Design, and Evaluation of Personal Indexes

In previous chapters, different types of indexes were described and discussed in terms of their advantages and disadvantages. In this chapter, techniques for determining index requirements for anticipated index uses will be covered. Once these index requirements have been specified, the requirements are matched against the characteristics of potentially usable indexes—the indexes that have been discussed in the previous chapters. The remainder of the chapter is devoted to a discussion of steps that should be taken prior to the preparation of the selected index and to the evaluation of the index once it has been prepared.

DETERMINING INDEX NEEDS

At the risk of being redundant, let us restate once again the objectives of an index. These objectives are to assist the index user in locating documents and, ultimately, the information contained in the documents and to do so in response to a need for information. The objectives

111

should be achieved with a reasonable expenditure of time and effort for the over-all operation of preparing and using the index. Unless these objectives are achieved within a reasonable time and with a reasonable expenditure of effort, the potential index user will go elsewhere for his information or perhaps go without it. The "elsewhere" may be a published index in the library, a knowledgeable colleague, or the laboratory where the work is repeated. We cannot specify what a reasonable time and effort may be for an individual; this is a subjective judgment. Also, the justification for an index and the specification of the index for a researcher's document collection is dependent on the nature of the researcher's document collection and on how he intends to use it. This is what we shall now discuss.

One characteristic of the researcher's document collection, its size, can be dealt with very quickly. We are assuming that the collection is above a certain critical size, say several hundred documents. Anything smaller than this does not really require an index since most of us can locate documents from a collection of this size without an index. We have also stipulated that the researcher's document collection is going to be smaller than about 10,000 documents. Document collections that are much larger than this are usually not found in researchers' offices. It should be pointed out that we are referring to the size of the collection as anticipated five or ten years from now, with expected additions as well as deletions by voluntary or involuntary withdrawals. The preparation of an index does take time and we would, therefore, want it to be usable for a few years. The adequacy of the collection and its use are the two other important characteristics. Knowledge of these characteristics will help us in determining what type of index or types of indexes to prepare. It may also suggest that no index should be prepared. Documents are collected because we anticipate a need for them in the near or distant future. Why collect documents otherwise? (The question is mostly, though not entirely, rhetorical. There are interior decorators who suggest the purchase of handsomely bound books by the foot, not to have them read but to add to the elegance of the decor of a house. We can hardly justify the collection of documents in a reseacher's office for this purpose.) How and how frequently the document collection is used are thus basic questions in determining index needs. We are in a better position to answer these questions for an index to be used primarily by an individual researcher than for an index that is prepared for a large and possibly heterogeneous group of users. Still there are problems. Let us mention two: It requires some self-discipline to keep a record of document use for a period of time. There is no precise technique for translating records of use into types of indexes that are best for each type of use. Only general guidelines "learned on the job" are available and we will discuss these guidelines shortly.

Almost any type of access point can be provided in an index but whether or not it should be provided depends on anticipated index use. If, as was mentioned in the last chapter, the index is used frequently to gather documents written by friends prior to their visits, then access points for author-friends might be appropriate. If we wish to use the index to retrieve amusing anecdotes for enlivening dry lectures, then access points by funny stories would be suitable for a particular document collection. Any type of access point is appropriate as long as its cost of preparation is justified by its use. There is also another factor of index use—the researcher's memory and mental habits. If he has a photographic memory, chances are that he will not need an index. Unfortunately, most of us are not so blessed and we need memory aids. If we remember certain things about documents, such as journal titles, then journal titles might be good access points or memory aids for our index.

The shopper for a new index may find himself in one of two circumstances: he may have an index with which he is dissatisfied or he may have an unindexed document collection that he would like to have indexed. When no index exists, ways in which such an index would be used need to be determined. In both instances, records of document use should be collected to provide the data on which to base a decision as to the type of index that is to be prepared. Case histories of use of the document collection should therefore be assembled in sufficient number and over a sufficient period of time to provide the necessary data. A suggested order of magnitude figure is 50 uses of the documents to be collected over a period of, say, 6 months. A tape recorder might be a useful tool in collecting the case histories since this cuts down on the labor involved—less writing needs to be done by the researcher, assuming of course that someone will transcribe the record for him. Case histories of uses of the document collection consist of a record of the question and titles of documents selected as being relevant to the question. Such case histories should be gathered whether or not there is an index to the collection. The purpose of the collection of the case histories is to identify frequency of use of the collection as well as the typical use or uses of the collection. It is these typical uses that will be looked at for determining index requirements. This is because economics dictate that we prepare the index for the typical or common type of use of the collection. We do not really have to concern ourselves too much with the exceptional types of uses. Those do not have to be handled as efficiently. When we talk about searches of the

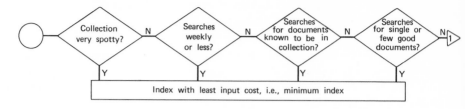

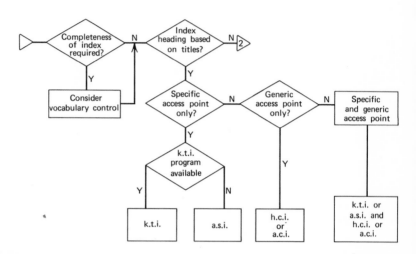

Figure 9-1. Flowchart for translating types of index use into types of indexes to be considered. *Symbols:* a.c.i = alphabetico-classified index; a.s.i. = alphabetic subject index; c.i. = coordinate index; h.c.i. = hierarchically classified index; k.t.i. = keyboard-from-title index.

index in this chapter we mean the typical or common uses of the index, the searches that we will attempt to handle most efficiently.

Let us now look at the collection and its typical use or uses and relate this information to the type of index or types of indexes that might be appropriate for such use. These characteristics are listed in the flow-chart given as Figure 9-1.

Adequacy of Researcher's Document Collection

The adequacy of the researcher's document collection is the first important factor in determining index requirements. Is the document or group of documents needed by the researcher usually in his document

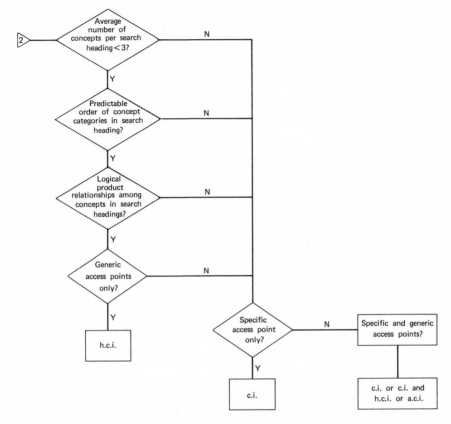

Figure 9-1 (*Continued*)

collection? If this is not the case and if he has to search indexes to other document collections, that is, the library, in addition to his own collection, the need for an index to the existing document collection may not be great. There may be a need to strengthen the document collection before any but a minimum index, an index with a single access point per document, is prepared.

Frequency of Use of Collection

A rarely used document collection may not deserve much time on indexing unless the rarity of use is caused by the absence of an index. If substantially fewer than 50 case histories of use were collected during the 6 months of index use study and if this is not because of the absence of an index, then a minimum index should be considered. A decision might also be made that no index is best if the collection has not been used extensively.

Nature of Index Use

The researcher may use his document collection for a variety of reasons. If it is primarily for retrieving a specific document known to be in his collection, then a minimum index might be adequate. This type of index may also be adequate if the typical search is only for a few documents with completeness of search results neither attempted nor required.

The four characteristics of the document collection and use just discussed are given in the flowchart in Figure 9-1. Notice that when any one of the questions is answered with a "yes," the preparation of a minimum index should be considered. If, on the other hand, the answer to each of the questions is "no," then something more than a minimum index may be appropriate. This brings us to other characteristics of typical document use. Let us again remind the reader that we are interested in the usual or typical type of use. We want to prepare an index that can handle the typical types of questions best even though it may not be particularly efficient for other types of questions.

Completeness of Search Results Required

This is not likely to be the typical search of the personal document for other than searches for a specific document. (When one retrieves that document one has 100% recall or completeness of search results.) There are two reasons for this: the typical search of any index is not a search for everything on a subject covered by the index and the researcher's document collection is usually not sufficiently inclusive to permit a complete search of everything that there is on the subject. Just in case the typical search is for everything on the subject included in the collection, an index vocabulary with vocabulary control should be considered. The alternative is to spend the time in the searching phase of the index. Neither alternative is satisfactory but since this is likely to be a hypothetical situation, we will not dwell on this matter.

Depth of Index

If the typical search can be successfully conducted with words selected or derived from the title, a relatively shallow index might be appropriate. The type of index to select depends on the types of access points that are anticipated. For searches with specific access points, a keyword-from-title index should be considered if the required computer program is available. The alternative is an alphabetic subject index. For search requests with generic access points, a hierarchically classified or an alphabetico-classified index should be considered. For searches that require both specific and generic access points, a combination of either keyword-from-title index or alphabetic subject index and hierarchically classified or alphabetico-classified index might be best.

It may be that a shallow index, one based on words from document titles, is not adequate for handling typical searches. When this is so, we will need to continue our search for an adequate index. Again, we will examine our typical search headings but now we will look for additional characteristics. These characteristics will be illustrated by means of the following search heading:

Preparation of flexible packages from a plastic material

There are four concepts in this search heading: "Preparation," "Flexible," "Packages," and "Plastic material." Each of these concepts, as well as other concepts in search headings, can be grouped under broad categories as was done in the preparation of subject authority lists discussed in Chapter 3 and as was done with faceted classification systems discussed in Chapter 8. In this search heading, we might group preparation under the process category, flexible under properties category, packages under the product category, the plastic materials under the materials category. The order of the search heading concept categories for our illustrated search heading is therefore process, properties, product, and materials. Other orders are also possible and the anticipated order of concept categories in the typical search headings is a factor in the selection of an index. The four concepts are connected in a logical product relationship since we are looking for documents that mention preparation, *and* flexible, *and* packages, *and* plastic materials. Headings with concepts related as logical sums, logical differences, or combination of logical products, sums, and differences are also possible. The nature of the logical relationships among concepts in an index heading also has a bearing on the choice of an index. Finally, we need to look at the specificity of both the access point as well as the other concepts in the search heading. In our example, all three concepts are relatively generic. The fourth concept, flexibility, might be considered specific. A more specific search heading would be the molding of flexible packages from plastic materials; an even more specific heading would be the molding of flexible bottle caps from polyethylene. Let us now discuss these effects of search heading variables on the choice of index as indicated in the flowchart.

Number of Concepts per Search Heading

The number of concepts in index headings of conventional indexes—the alphabetic subject index, the hierarchically classified index, and the alphabetico-classified index—is usually limited to three or less. More than three concepts per index heading are unusual, particularly for the hierarchically classified index in which the same concept may be expressed two or more times at different levels of specificity. This is because conventional index headings with more than three concepts are both awkward to prepare and to search. There is no such restriction with coordinate indexes. As many concepts as necessary can be combined at the time of the search to form search headings. It is for this reason that coordinate indexes should be given an edge for typical search headings of three or more concepts.

Order of Search Headings

If the order of concept categories in search headings can be predicted, the required order can be provided in the conventional index headings. If most anticipated searches are for concepts in, for example, process, properties, and product order then that particular order is provided in the index headings of conventional indexes. When no particular concept order is predominant, then a conventional index is at a disadvantage over coordinate indexes since either all possible concept orders need to be provided (which makes for an index that is bulkier and more time consuming to prepare) or if only certain orders of concept categories are prepared (which makes for a more time-consuming index to search when the desired order of concept category is not available). If the latter option is taken, one can lead the user to the selected concept categories order by means of cross-references (called chain indexes in the case of the faceted classification system). This, however, is not a satisfactory solution to the problem. We have some evidence that chain indexes are awkward to use. Once again, the coordinate index is at an advantage when the order of concept categories in search headings cannot be predicted. There is no ordering problem in a coordinate index. Each of the concepts are access points and each concept can be coordinated with any other concept to form a search heading at the time of the search.

Logical Relationship Among Concepts in Search Heading

The typical logical relationship among concepts in conventional index headings is the logical product relationship. If other than logical product relationships among concepts in search headings are required, particularly if this requirement cannot be anticipated at the time of indexing, the coordinate index is at an advantage. Any logical relationship among concepts can be provided with coordinate indexes at the time of the search of the index, although some logical relationships require multiple-step searches with some of these indexes.

Specificity of Search Headings

If the typical search headings are generic, consist of fewer than three concepts in a logical product relationship and are in an order that can be determined at the time of indexing, a hierarchically classified index might be appropriate. When this is not the case, a coordinate index is probably preferable. This can be a coordinate index that is used for both specific and generic searches. Generic searches can be conducted in coordinate indexes by coordinating specific concept descriptors in logical sum order, for example, a search for the generic concept plastic would be done by searching under polyethylene, or polypropylene, or polystyrene, or other specific plastics. Another way of conducting generic searches with coordinate indexes is to look for all of the documents indexed under one generic concept descriptor. If both specific and generic searches are typical searches, a combination coordinate index with the filing of documents under broad subjects (a combination discussed in the last chapter) might be more appropriate than just having a coordinate index.

We have not mentioned author indexes, faceted classification systems, and citation indexes in this chapter, but will do so now. If author searches are exclusively or frequently conducted, then author indexes with or without subject indexes should be prepared. Faceted classification systems are worthy of consideration when the subjects of the documents to be indexed can be characterized in terms of a small number of words and phrases of a controlled index vocabulary and when the flexibility of searching under different orders of concept categories is not required. Citation indexes, either by themselves or in combination with word indexes, should be considered when the citation network in a given field is good enough to provide access to relevant documents and when the researcher likes to do his searches in this way.

REVIEW OF CHARACTERIZATION OF INDEXES

We are concerned with indexes to document collections of up to 10,000 documents. All but one of the indexes which have been discussed can be used for document collections of this size. The exception is the coordinate index on edge-notched cards which tends to become cumbersome for collections larger than 5,000 documents. What about the cost of index preparation? The intellectual cost in time for familiarizing oneself with a document is the same for each type of index as long as the depth of the index is the same. It takes as long to read an abstract for an alphabetic subject index as for a coordinate index. The reading of the document or a portion of the document need not be done for a keyword-in-context index based on document titles only or for a citation index, but familiarization with the document would still be necessary to determine whether or not to include the document in the collection. It will take several minutes per document to translate the indexable information into the language of the index if a controlled index vocabulary is to be used and if a post-coordinated or pre-coordinated index is used. This step does not apply for citation indexes and usually not for keyword-from-title indexes. The physical preparation of index units for the three forms of coordinate indexes, the Uniterm index, the optical coincidence index, and the edge-notched card index, with an average of 8 descriptors per document, takes about 5 minutes per document. Since a separate physical unit must be prepared for each use of a pre-coordinate index heading for a document, the physical unit preparation time for this type of index is likely to be somewhat longer, the incremental time being dependent on the amount of information to be recorded on each index unit. It is also somewhat longer, about 7 minutes per document, for a keyword-from-title index of lesser depth, about 5 access points per document. Computer processing time must be added to this figure. The preparation of index units for the citation index is likely to be the slowest process if we take the average of about 14 cited references per indexed document. The reader should count on spending at least 10 minutes for indexing a document with each of the indexes except the citation index which may take longer unless the citations are highly abbreviated. It should be remembered that about half of this time is for clerical tasks that may be delegated.

SETTING UP THE INDEX

Let us assume that we have selected a particular type of index and that we are ready for the next stage in the process. This is the planning or get-ready stage. At this stage we will plan the over-all index-ing operation to make the best use of the researcher's time and any clerical or other assistant's time that might be available to the researcher. We will review the steps in preparing an index, steps that were listed in Chapter 2, and discuss some of the decisions that need to be made. The discussion is in general terms so that it can be applicable to any type of index that might have been selected.

Inclusion of Documents in Index

A decision needs to be made on the inclusion and exclusion of documents that are now in the collection as well as for documents that will be added to the collection. Should all of the documents that are now in the collection be included in the index? If the answer to this question is no, can documents be excluded on the basis of form of publication (e.g., correspondence, books), or on the basis of date of publication, (e.g., any document published before a certain date), or by subject (e.g., subjects on which relatively little is in the collection), or by any combination of these factors? A "halfway" decision may also be made for the less useful documents. If a multiple-access-points-per-document index is to be prepared for documents of primary interest, a single access point index may be prepared for the other documents. The collection may also be enriched by adding documents on subjects of primary interest before the index is started. A similar set of decisions needs to be made for newly received and current documents. There is also the possibility of including in the index documents that are of interest to the researcher but that are not in his collection.

Selection of Indexable Information

Is the indexable information selected on the basis of document titles, abstracts, or specified portions of text? Is the indexable information se-lected exclusively on the basis of today's research interests or can antici-pated broadening or narrowing of research interests be taken into con-sideration? Is the indexable information recorded on the document itself or copied onto a worksheet? If the indexable information is copied onto a worksheet, can categories of indexable information or commonly used index headings be printed on the worksheet both to save indexer's time and to increase the consistency of the index? The indexing consistency might also be increased if the rules for indexing (what to index and how to index) are formulated before the index is started and if these rules are included in a manual of operations.

Selection of Filing Point for Indexed Document

This can either be done at the time the indexable information for the document is selected in case the document is filed by subject, or prior to the selection of indexable information if the document is to be filed by accession number or name of author. In the latter case, the selection of the filing point can be delegated to a clerk.

Preparation of Index Entries and Merging of Index Entries

The index heading is either the individual unit of indexable information (the word or phrase selected in scanning the document) or the unit of indexable information translated into the standard index heading with the help of the subject authority list, in case a controlled index vocabulary is used. The physical preparation of the index entry (the index heading plus the document identification and/or filing point) can be delegated to a clerk in either case. The researcher needs only to be involved when new decisions are required for translating indexable information into index headings, that is, when decisions for translating a given unit of indexable information have not as yet been recorded in the subject authority list. Proofing and editing by the researcher of index entries is desirable for greater index consistency. The newly prepared index entries that are merged with existing index entries should also be edited by the researcher. At that point in the operation, additional cross-references to related index entries might be made by him— this, again, to increase the consistency of the index.

Filing of Indexed Documents

There are several physical means of filing documents. Documents can be placed in file folders which in turn are placed in file cabinets. Documents can also be filed in pamphlet boxes, cardboard boxes of varying sizes, that are usually filed on bookshelves. Special containers may be required for oversized material such as maps and engineering drawings or for nonprint materials as exemplified by records, tapes, microforms, or slides. A list of suppliers for such special containers is found in buyers' guides that are available in libraries.[1] File folders, index cards, and boxes for index cards can be purchased in stationery stores.

There is a related matter that might be brought up at this point. If the researcher's document collection is used exclusively by him, then no formal charge out procedure is required. The researcher pulls out the documents from his file, puts them someplace else for use and, hopefully, returns the documents to their original location when he is finished with them. If the researcher's document collection is used by groups of individuals (e.g., students), then some more formalized procedure for charging out the documents might be advisable. The simplest procedure is to insert in the place of the borrowed document a sheet on which is recorded the name of the borrower, the document identification, and the date. This will still not guarantee the return of the document but it will give the researcher a record of who might have it.

INDEX EVALUATION

Once you have started the preparation of an index, you will probably want to know how good it is. But this is difficult to determine. For one thing, you will not be able to conduct a meaningful test of the index until you have a substantial portion of your document collection included in it. A test of an index to, say, 100 documents is likely to be inconclusive. If you cannot select documents that you are trying to locate in the test of a collection of 100 documents, you can safely conclude that the index will not get better when more documents are included in it. If, on the other hand, the tests are successful for the size of the collection used in the test, you cannot extrapolate the results to a larger index. But let us assume that you have your entire collection indexed. Can you test the goodness of the index at that point? The answer is a qualified yes, but the effort involved in the test may not be justified for these reasons. To test an index for ability to retrieve relevant documents you need to know the relevant documents that should be retrieved in the test questions. This is usually not the case. You can get around this problem by either using artificial questions with known relevant documents (and run the possibility of meaningless test results) or you can go over each of the documents in the collection to determine whether or not it is relevant to the test questions. The second alternative is very time consuming and not really satisfactory. You should have gotten the message by now that any index is likely to yield only a portion of relevant documents that are included in it. Not only that, the index will probably yield nonrelevant documents as well as an incomplete set of relevant documents. What recall and precision ratios, as defined in Chapter 2, are considered good in terms of search results? We do not have any standards and simply do not know at this point.[2] It depends mostly on what you consider to be adequate for your needs. And that brings us to a basic point. Index evaluation is subjective at this time and might well remain so for the foreseeable future. What does this mean in terms of the evaluation of your own index? The index should be looked at in terms of anticipated as well as actual indexing time per document, search time per typical search, satisfaction with search results based on your knowledge of the collection, and frequency of use. If any of these factors appear out of balance—if the indexing time is considerably higher than anticipated, if it takes much longer to search the index than anticipated, if a document known to be in the collection cannot be retrieved, and if the index is not used as frequently as was anticipated—then a second look should be taken at the entire operation.

SUMMARY

In this chapter we have looked at a number of steps that need to be taken before and during the preparation of indexes. These steps include the examination of uses of documents to be included in the index so that we can determine what type of index or types of indexes are most appropriate for anticipated index use. There are circumstances where the best index is the absence of an index and this should be kept in mind. If a decision has been made to prepare an index, a number of steps have to be taken in the planning of the index and its preparation. Finally, some comments were made on the evaluation of indexes. The message is that we lack objective measuring sticks for the evaluation of indexes but that there are subjective measures that we should put to use. In the next and last chapter, we look ahead a few years and speculate what a personal index might be like in the near future. This look into the future is intended to assist in the selection of a personal index.

REFERENCES

1. For example, the *Library Journal* has an annual purchasing guide in which the names and addresses of suppliers of pamphlet boxes, boxes for slides, microforms, records, and other filing supplies needed for indexes are listed.
2. This matter is discussed by Rees in his review of work on the evaluation of information storage and retrieval systems. Rees points out that more is involved than searching a set of test documents against a set of test questions. There are real methodological problems that we have not as yet resolved. Rees, A. M., "Evaluation of Information Systems and Services," *Annual Review of Information Science and Technology*, 2:63–86 (1967).

Chapter Ten

Information Storage and Retrieval Systems of the Future

In this chapter we discuss some of the technological developments that may affect users of personal indexes not today, but perhaps five or more years from now. The question may well be raised whether it would not be better to wait a few years if an index that is prepared today will become obsolescent in the near future. This question is posed at the beginning of the chapter to clear up possible misunderstandings. Inherent in the question is the assumption that something obsolescent is no longer useful. This is not necessarily so. The owner of a house with a kitchen of the 1940's may find his appliances perfectly satisfactory even though his appliance dealer may want to convince him otherwise. There is an analogy with indexes. An index may not make use of the latest equipment or latest technique but it may be completely adequate under certain specified conditions.

Let us, however, go beyond the indexing systems that we described in previous chapters and discuss an indexing system that makes use of technological developments that are either here today or are anticipated. The system that will be called the idealized system is something like the push-button system mentioned in Chapter 1, only more so. It resembles systems described in a report of a planning study on information transfer experiments[1] and in a book on the libraries of tomorrow by Licklider.[2] We should emphasize that such a system does not now exist on an operational basis, although we have some reason to believe that it might come into being in the future.

The user of our idealized system will be sitting at his own terminal which is conveniently located in his own office. The terminal will be both an input (querying) station to a network of computers and an output (answering) station. The output station receives messages from the computer network as well as enlarged microforms of documents sent from libraries some distance removed. The computers will have in their memory surrogates of all of the documents that are of interest to the individual user of the system. The surrogates are the bibliographic citations, abstracts, and index headings of the corresponding documents. The index headings will include subjects, authors, citations, dates, forms of publication, and any other types of access points that might be useful. This will be an index of great depth with more subject headings per document than in indexes now in use. For searching the index, the user queries the system in a language that resembles everyday, natural language. He can readjust his query if the results of the first step of the search are not satisfactory, which is likely to be the case. Rapid feedback from the computer is available to facilitate the negotiation of questions. The initial output from the computer might be an indication of the number of documents on file for a particular request. After the question has been negotiated, the bibliographic citations of potentially relevant documents with or without index headings or abstracts will be displayed at the terminal. All, or a portion, of the potentially relevant documents can then be ordered on another screen of the terminal. The user will have an option of making hard copies from the images on the screen, although this option will probably not be used extensively. Why bother to keep a file of documents when it is so easy to call for them by means of the index and screening mechanism? The system will also include indexes to documents that are only in the researcher's office, documents such as letters, minutes of meetings, or lecture notes. The index to these documents will be stored in a section of the computer's memory that is dedicated for this purpose and can only be approached by the researcher.

So far we have only mentioned the use of the system for making searches of documents that may contain answers to questions. There are other features. The computer will have in its memory tables of numeric data that are now consulted through handbooks and other printed data compilations. For this use, the system is not queried for documents that may be of potential interest (document retrieval) but for questions that can be answered with a number or a series of numbers (data or fact retrieval). A current awareness service will also be included and it is intended to assist the individual researcher in keeping up to date on new publications in his areas of interest. The individual user of the system will characterize his research interests in the language of the index, that is, his research interests will be indexed just like another document in the system. The index headings for new documents entering the system will be matched against the index headings that represent individual researchers' professional interests. When matches occur, potentially useful documents will be directed to the researcher's attention via his terminal.

The idealized system consists, as do all systems for that matter, of a combination of components—people, equipment, instructions for using the equipment, documents, and surrogates of documents—all put together to perform a specified task. Some of these components are available today, others are available on an experimental basis only, and still others are in what might be broadly called the non-ready stage. Let us examine the status of these components.

HARDWARE COMPONENTS OF SYSTEM

We will need computers that are used on an on-line, time-shared basis, something that is in existence today. Licklider points out that at the end of 1967, 50 such computer systems were in commercial use.[3] If the system is to include an index to a large document collection, which would undoubtedly be the case, then we will need a computer system with large storage capacity. Here again, significant progress was made in 1967. In that year, IBM announced the availability of a storage device that holds one trillion (10^{17}) bits. This is two or three orders of magnitude larger than the next largest digital storage device in existence.[4] We lack system specifications to determine how much storage capacity is required for our system, or more likely our network of systems, but this trillion-bit memory should go a long way toward providing the required storage capacity. Even though output devices are getting faster and more versatile than the teletypewriter units that were used exclusively when on-line computer use was first introduced, there is reason to believe that our idealized system will make use of the computer memory for the storage of document surrogates and photographic storage for storing documents. The limiting speed here is not that of the output terminal but that of the human reader. Too much computer and computer terminal time is likely to be used if we attempt to match human reading speed with computer printout speed. There is another reason for separating the storage of documents and document surrogates. Computer storage of pictures and illustrations in multiple colors is still not on the horizon. Instead, we will store the documents on microform at some distance away from the terminal, in one or more designated libraries. Enlargements of potentially relevant documents will be sent "over the wire" (by telefacsimile transmission) and displayed on a screen that is part of the researcher's terminal. Use of telefacsimile equipment has been made for a number of years in newspaper offices as well as in libraries. Today's equipment for viewing enlargements of microforms, either sent by telefacsimile transmission or physically inserted into the microform reader, leaves much to be desired. The quality of the image projected on the microfilm reader's screen will have to be improved if the researcher is to read documents in this form for extensive periods of time. Work aimed at the improvement of this equipment is now being conducted by Project INTREX which does make use of computers for on-line searching of an index and the transmission of microforms of documents that are enlarged on a screen at the user's terminal.[5]

NON-HARDWARE COMPONENTS OF SYSTEM

There are several non-hardware problems to be resolved in our idealized system. Three such problems are bibliographic control, indexing, and man-machine communications.

Bibliographic Control

Before a document collection can be indexed, it must be assembled and then, if it is a continuing project, kept up-to-date. This is not easy to do for subjects on which much has been and will continue to be written. Documents on a broad subject, such as chemistry, are published by universities, societies, government agencies, and commercial organizations. These documents are in the form of preprints, conference proceedings, journal articles, patents, and reports, or theses, in the case of records of original research. Sometimes the same document is published in two or more forms. Secondary publications (condensations of the original documents) are published in abstract journals, reviews, texts, encyclopedias, or handbooks. The variety of sources, forms, and types of publications causes problems in bibliographic control if attempts are made to collect all documents on a particular subject. The federal government has been interested in this problem for a number of years and has commissioned several studies of it. A number of plans for a national system of document handling in science and technology have been proposed.[6] As of 1969, these plans represent work toward, rather than achievement of, bibliographic control in science and technology. Other subjects are not even at this stage. There are no insurmountable problems in the way of achieving bibliographic control. Agreement on a plan and the necessary effort for its implementation are required. This will take time.

Indexing

The indexes that are now in use, the ones that have been discussed in previous chapters, have a number of shortcomings. These shortcomings become more apparent (as well as more serious) when the indexes are used for the organization of large document collections. There are several good reasons for these shortcomings. The indexer must select index headings based on anticipated use of the documents, yet he cannot predict with any degree of certainty how a document will be used in the future. At any rate, there are many more ways in which a document can be requested and used than can be provided in an index. The indexer is restricted by necessity to a limited number of particular ways of characterizing a document and his work is also restricted by what is known about the subject of the document at the time of indexing. This way of looking at the document and the knowledge of the subject of the document are likely to change and what might have been an unimportant aspect of a document at the time of indexing may become important at the time the document is sought in the index. The indexer introduces other biases into the system. He may not know enough about the subject of the documents that he is indexing or he may know too much about them (and perhaps treat everything as "old hat"). Since he is human, he is certain to be inconsistent in making his index decisions. How can these problems be solved in the idealized indexing system? An author could be asked (or told by his editor) to index documents that he has written. This may reduce the cost of preparing an index, but may or may not result in a better index and one in which the aforementioned problems would be avoided. While the author-indexer would know more about the documents he indexes than the professional indexer, he may lack the indexer's skills in preparing the index headings as well as the motivation for doing so. The problem of bias of indexing from the point of view of the time the document was written and the problem of inconsistency would still be present with author-prepared indexes. There is also the problem of finding enough indexers to do the job, particularly if it is not a glamorous and high-paying job, which it probably will not be. What about using a computer to do the indexing? Computers have been used to index documents on the basis of titles in the previously discussed keyword-from-title indexes. Can computers be used for the preparation of indexes of greater depth, based on abstracts or full texts of documents? Work is being done along this line but it is still experimental, presently restricted to small collections of 1000 or fewer documents.[7] We can anticipate computer-prepared indexes, refined by human indexers in the idealized system since work on machine translations has given us an indication that in at least the foreseeable future the machine is not to be left completely to its own devices with such work.

Man-machine Communications

This is really a difficult problem. We have been facing it in man-man communications when librarians are answering reference questions for a patron. This has been, and is still, an art rather than a science, and it cannot be described formally. But we need to know more about the process if we are going to reproduce it on the computer. We lack, at this time, the necessary knowledge of how the user of the index will phrase and refine his questions and how he will want to interact with the system. A considerable amount of experimentation is required in this area. Once we know what the dialogue between man and machine should be, we will have to instruct machines how to conduct this dialogue. In a recent review on this subject, Licklider expresses some optimism that such programs can be prepared if we are willing to expend the necessary resources.[8] Salton takes a more cautious view on this matter.[9]

There are other problems to be faced before our idealized system can go on stream. Copyright is certainly one of them. As the contents of documents become available on demand from systems such as the one being described, commercial publishers as well as societies who need subscription revenue to carry out their publication program will have a smaller market for their publications. They can be expected to object and they should be compensated for lost revenue in some manner. There is also the privacy problem. The use of the indexes can be and will probably be monitored by those wishing to learn more about the information needs and to use the information for making necessary improvements in the system. The index user will have to be convinced that such monitoring is not being done with any ulterior motives, and that when he needs or wants to conduct private searches he may do so. These and related problems are discussed in a review of information networks by Becker and Olsen.[10] Again we do not have insurmountable problems but problems that will take time to resolve.

The closest thing to this idealized system now in existence is Project TIP at M.I.T., an on-line computer-searched index to a portion of the physics literature. The system has been in operation since January 1966 and in 1967 contained about 60,000 documents from 32 physics journals. An IBM 7094 with about 150 consoles (standard IBM 1050 keyboards) is used. Search instructions resemble natural language and are easy to learn. Searches can be done by author, location of author, keywords in titles, and citations. The system also includes personal document collections of individual researchers. Kessler, who developed and is operating the system, comments that a vast array of problems is appearing in the use of the system, problems that have to do with people as consumers of scientific information, their needs, habits, and prejudices.[11] Three other organizations have announced plans for on-line computer-searched indexes to researchers' document collections.[12]

We will hedge our bets somewhat by letting the reader decide for himself if and when something like the idealized system will arrive. Predictions of the future are notoriously hazardous, particularly in a field such as this one in which timing does not only depend on technological developments but also on the system's users. They have to invest a considerable amount of money and manpower to bring about this system and this money and manpower will surely be in demand for other purposes.

Yet there are aspects of the information problem about which we can be more definite. The problem will get worse rather than better as more researchers write more papers and as computers are used to grind out reports. During the next few years, relatively few researchers are likely to be served with on-line computer-searched indexes to their document collections and/or the published literature at large. It would, therefore, stand to reason that if a researcher needs an index to his document collection now he should not wait for a greatly improved system that might not be ready for several more years. Instead he should consider using the types of indexes that were discussed in previous chapters. There are important fringe benefits to having the user involved with the design, preparation, and use of an index to his document collection. He is likely to become more knowledgeable in the problems of index preparation as well as index use. Such knowledge by the final user of the information is badly needed by index designers who have had largely to do without it in the past. There is a very real need for the final user of the information to participate in the development of indexing or other information systems that are intended for him.

His involvement might indeed be considered a matter of enlightened self-interest. The final user of this information will have an important role in the development of information systems. This can either be a passive role or an active role. It is our hope that the user will participate actively in the development of information systems since it is our belief that he has much to gain in doing so.

REFERENCES

1. Overhage, C. F. J. and Harman, R. J., eds., *INTREX. Report of a Planning Conference on Information Transfer Experiments.* Cambridge, Mass.: M.I.T. Press, 1965.
2. Licklider, J. C. R., *Libraries of the Future.* Cambridge, Mass.: M.I.T. Press, 1965.
3. Licklider, J C. R., "Man-Computer Communication," *Annual Review of Information Science and Technology,* 3:232 (1968).
4. *Ibid.,* p. 221.
5. Massachusetts Institute of Technology Project Intrex, Semi-Annual Activity Report, September 15, 1967 to March 15, 1968. M.I.T., Cambridge, Mass., 1968.
6. Carter, L. F., et al., *National Document Handling Systems for Science and Technology.* New York: John Wiley, 1967.
7. The most extensive description of work on machine-prepared indexes is in a book by Salton who has done extensive work in this field. Salton, G., *Automatic Information Organization and Retrieval.* New York: McGraw-Hill, 1968.
8. Licklider, J. C. R., "Man-Computer Communication," *Annual Review of Information Science and Technology,* 3:226 (1968).
9. Salton believes that the transition from automatic reference retrieval system based on the identification of only the principal concepts attached to each stored document and on the processing of single type of search request, to automatic question answering systems using a more complete analysis and more sophisticated search and retrieval methods is not an easy one to make and that the outlook for the development of such systems in the foreseeable future is not good. (Salton, G., *Automatic Information Organization and Retrieval.* New York: McGraw-Hill, 1968, pp. 412–413).
10. Becker, J. and Olsen, W. C., "Information Networks," *Annual Review of Information Science and Technology,* 3:289–327 (1968).
11. Kessler, M. M., "The On-Line Technical Information System at M.I.T.— Project TIP," *IEEE International Convention Record.* Institute of Electrical and Electronic Engineers, N.Y., 1967. Part 10, pp. 40–43.
12. The following three articles describe plans for experiments with on-line computer searched indexes to personal document collections: Heaps, D. M. and Sorenson, P., "An On-Line Personal Documentation System, *Proceedings of the American Society for Information Science,* vol. 5, pp. 201–207, 1968; Systems Development Corp., *Research and Technology Division Report for 1967,* Santa Monica, Cal., Section 4, p. 11; Walker, D. E., "SAFARI, An On-Line Text Processing System," *Proceedings of the American Documentation Institute Annual Meeting,* vol. 4, pp. 144–147, 1967.

Index

The index to this book is an alphabetic subject index. The individual subject headings (mostly nouns or noun phrases in singular form) are arranged in one alphabet with no inversion of phrases. The alphabetization is letter by letter rather than word by word (Indexing system is filed before Index preparation) to the first comma. *See* and *See also* cross-references are provided to lead the user to the selected index headings and to provide a path among related index headings. Parenthetical statements are included to avoid ambiguity. For example, the word "Subject" was added after the heading "History, index vocabulary" to indicate that index vocabulary in the field of history is referred to rather than the history of index vocabularies. The index contains both subject headings and author headings.

Access points are mostly for types of indexes, index components, and index variables. Chemistry, history, and other subject areas are given as access points to direct the reader to case histories of personal index use or index vocabularies in his area of interest.